A Million Reason

As George Müller did before us, we prayed and trusted God daily for our...

PROVISIONS

A True Story of Divine Care

Stephen L. Meeks

ISBN-10:1494774038

Published by Clipper Ships Enterprises, LLC

5279 Highway 297

Pioneer, TN 37847

Most Scripture quotations are from New International Version (NIV) Holy Bible, © 1973, 1978, 1984 by Biblica, Inc. Bold and comments in parenthesis are added and mine. References from other translations are noted in the text. In some instances I have paraphrased Scripture references.

INTRODUCTION

Place a pebble in a bag. Its weight is negligible. Continue, daily, over twenty-five years to add pebbles, and the bag becomes quite heavy.

If we had received only one gift in answer to prayer, or even two or three, it could easily be dismissed as coincidence or a fluke; but we have documented hundreds of accounts of God's provisions in answer to specific prayers. Taken collectively, they are weighty evidence that God is present, hearing prayer, and active in the world.

Some might assume that this task of trusting God for our supplies, though admittedly challenging, has been a burden to us. At times, it seemed so, but I have come to relax comfortably in His ever-tender, ever-present, ever-reliable care. George Müller spoke to this agreeing with Jesus' assurance of God's care, saying, "Not a sparrow falls from heaven unmarked by the All-seeing eye..." [1]

Provisions chronicles more than a quarter-century of obeying a perceived call to totally rely in prayer on God for daily provisions, and the inexplicable things that happened as a result.

"Even the daily bread, by which our bodies are sustained, and for which we are taught to pray, is, as it were, manna sent us directly from Heaven. Yet our provision looks to superficial observers, as in so many respects, like the ordinary manna, that they are apt to mistake it, and that even we ourselves in our unbelief too often forget the daily dispensation of our bread from heaven."
-Alfred Edersheim [2]

---

1 William Henry Harding, *The Life of George Müller: A Record of Faith Triumphant* (London: Morgan, 1914), p 287.

2 Alfred Eidersheim, *Bible History: Old Testament* (Massachusetts: Hendrickson Publishers, Inc., 1995), p 96.

It is with all my heart that I dedicate *Provisions* to Donna -- my wife, my friend, my companion in the Gospel, and God's greatest blessing to me.

You have willingly lived each moment, and taken every step of this journey with me; none of it would have happened if you had not. Therefore, we are all grateful, and deeply indebted to you.

ACKNOWLEDGEMENTS

"A book cannot know what words will be written upon its pages;
a man cannot know what acts God may perform in his life."
–Stephen 1999

Dear Reader,

No true-life story is lived alone; there are many contributors to every narrative. In fact, hundreds of obedient Saints, knowingly or not, penned a line, wrote a paragraph, or crafted a chapter in *Provisions*. I have protected the identities of many of those who sent gifts, made donations, or helped us by using initials, pseudonyms, or other references instead of their actual names. Many incidents and individuals - equally as important in making our testimony possible - have not been included only due to space and time limitations. However, neither my wife, Donna, nor I could have survived, ministered, or provided this testimony without the faithful responses to God's nudging each of them. Because of a collective obedience, lives have been changed, and now, it is highly likely that yours will be also.

I owe a debt of gratitude to several who have helped produce this book. My son, Caleb, has been a consultant on many levels. My neighbor, Steve Greek, and my former co-worker, Oneal Tankersley, were constant and affirming encouragers from the start. I owe a very special "thank you" to my faithful brothers and friends on the Board of Directors of GoodSoil Ministries, Inc. They stood behind me, walked with me through the most difficult decisions, and held my feet to the fire when I wavered.

Through its several renditions, a number of friends have invested personally in editing, revising, proofing, illustrating, and strengthening this material. Janet Allison, Nancy Robb, Martha J. Provost, Marcy Bryan, Lisa Meeks, Dr. Albert Lemmons (prayermatters.org), and especially my wife, Donna, deserve special merit in Glory for their hours of attention to the details, comments, and prayers. I appreciate each of them so much!

For a second time now, I offer my appreciation to Brooklyn Sims for her formatting and design work that makes reading the material both easy and beautiful. You're gifted!

Lastly, a word to and about my wife, Donna. God talked to Abraham and he obeyed because he trusted God's will. Sarah, on the other hand, heard from Abraham, not directly from God, and she lived trusting Abraham's understanding of God's will. Certainly, Sarah had the more difficult challenge. Many times a wife has been called to trust her husband's discernment of God's will for her and their family. Donna, like Sarah, has trustingly followed me through these years of trusting God for provisions. Her 'calling' has been to follow her husband and not give in to fear (1 Peter 3:6), and to her great credit, she has not given in. Faith in God is challenging, but faith in a man who believes he is following God is challenging on a whole other level! If either of us has shown great faith, it has been Donna. Hers has been the more difficult work; therefore, *Provisions* is dedicated to her.

In a few hours, when you have turned the final page, pause. Quietly, contemplatively, be still. Briefly sit before the Heavenly Father. There, listen. If He calls you to any action, allow Him to fill the pages of your life. It will be a story all of us will want to hear, since He pens the most wonderful things.

All things by prayer; by prayer, all things.

Stephen L. Meeks

CONTENTS

NOTE TO THE READER

Comments and asides were added in italics to aid flow, provide clarity, and give context. In many instances, initials or pseudonyms were used in place of real names to protect the privacy of those involved. Any alteration to an entry was for the purpose of making a grammatical correction or to limit length to what's most pertinent to the story. The entire account is true.

MEETING MÜLLER

"I have seen something else under the sun: The race is not to the swift or the battle to the strong, nor does food come to the wise or wealth to the brilliant or favor to the learned; but time and chance happen to them all."
-Ecclesiastes 9:11

We are susceptible to the coincidence that can reformulate all our tomorrows. The writer C. S. Lewis admits that he was profoundly shaped by the random purchase of the George MacDonald novel <u>Phantastes</u>. Lewis later described how those first hours with MacDonald's words transported him on to an entirely new frontier.[3] Lewis' experience perfectly illustrates how a life can be profoundly changed by surprise -- ours was.

In my life prior to 1987, I had experienced a few occasions in which I could, and can, unflinchingly say that God answered my prayers. I'm sure these provided encouragement enough to push me farther into that realm.

The first three times I witnessed God act in my life were scattered across 15 years. The earliest was at age 12 after I had been immersed into Christ. I was excited to participate in the Communion. In our church's tradition, an offering

---

3 George MacDonald, *Phantastes : A Faerie Romance for Men and Women* (Massachusetts: Hendrickson Publishers, 2011).

was taken at the same time the Communion was served. I considered how much I should give. In a shoebox at the head of my bed, I kept all my money. My total life savings at that point was fifty cents.

I recall having spliced together two thoughts regarding giving: Jesus' words, "your righteousness should surpass that of the Pharisees," and what I must have heard from our preacher, that "Pharisees were known to give up to forty percent of their income." So, I decided I should give half of my money. It was a faith move, but I was committed to obeying God. Twenty-five cents would go in the offering plate.

On that Sunday, I gave my quarter. The next Sunday, I found that I had a dollar in my box; I gave half of it. The following week the wealth of my empire had grown to two dollars! Obediently, I gave half. I wish I'd kept that system going, but while I obviously did not make it onto the billionaire list with Gates and Zuckerberg, I still didn't come away empty-handed. I was learning that specifically when it came to financial care and provision, God was trustworthy.

As a senior in high school, God reinforced this to me when, looking ahead to college, I had decided to become a minister. That path meant seminary training, but my folks could not afford such an education. So, I decided to do my best to get an athletic scholarship. Mom had enrolled me in summer baseball since I was 11. Our high school team had some pretty good players, and I was one of them. In January three of us approached our coach, Terry Hopkins. "Coach, can we start practicing? We want to try for some scholarship money." He never looked up from his desk. "I can't do that. It's against league rules to start this early." We were bummed, but after a pause, he continued, "But the pitching machine is in the equipment room. If it is unlocked, I can't keep you from using it." My buddies and I grinned in understanding, delighted. Coach added, "Just put it back."

Well, it is no surprise that we found that door to be unlocked every afternoon until spring practice officially began. We had a history-making season. Our undefeated 12-0 record stands at Gladewater High School to this day. This advanced us to the regional playoff. For our size school, regional was the equivalent of the state championship! Unfortunately, we lost two out of three games at that level, but it was a thrilling run. My two buddies were offered full scholarships to Baylor University. Coach knew I wanted to attend a Christian college in Arkansas -- Harding College. He called their coaches for me. "Hey Meeks," he reported one day as we passed in the hall, "I called your school. They don't offer baseball scholarships." My heart broke. That night, finally alone, I knelt and cried beside my bed. "God, I have done all I knew to do. I want to do well. I want to be a minister, but now I don't know what to do. I'm sad, very sad. I have done everything I could. It's now up to you."

My options at that point were either to go to work sweeping floors at the factory where my dad worked, which would earn some money towards school in a year or two; or to work at Camp Deer Run as a staff member and influence kids, but the pay there was very little. It was a dilemma. At some point, I came to peace by deciding to work at camp. I thought, "Who knows, I may not live for two years. If not, I'll be more glad that I invested in the eternal lives of those kids than if I had a few thousand dollars saved toward college." So, I went to camp.

In the meantime, Coach Hopkins continued to make calls on my behalf and eventually contacted York College, a two-year Christian school in York, Nebraska. York did offer baseball scholarships, and they offered a partial one for me! I was excited. Though I was nervous about living so far from home, I was willing to leave home if it was God's path for me. It appeared that God had answered my prayers after all -- or so I thought.

The first weeks of summer raced by and the camp was entering its last session. I'd gotten a call on Saturday from Coach Small with York College saying he would soon be purchasing my airline tickets. As I sat at the camp gate the next day welcoming parents and campers, someone told me I had a phone call at the nurses' station. The only phone at camp was a landline at the nurses' station. Usually, phone calls meant trouble. I made my way to the phone and answered with trepidation, "Hello."

It was my dad. I knew there must be a REAL problem because my dad had never called me on a phone before in my entire life. To add to my panic, he started crying. I'd never known my dad to cry. He handed the phone to my mother.

She started, "Steve, are you okay?" This was typical of my mom, always concerned about the other person.

"Yea. I'm fine, what's wrong with Daddy?"

"Nothing, he is okay. We just got a call today from someone at church. Do you know Mrs. Lee?"

"No. I don't think so." I wondered why my dad was crying about a Mrs. Lee.

"Well, Mrs. Lee called, and she said that if you'd like to go to Harding, she'd pay your way."

I started crying too, and yelling, and jumping, and being really crazy and excited! The whole camp knew within a just a few minutes that I was going to Harding! God had done it. He answered my prayers and He even went beyond them. The enrollment that semester was the largest in the college's history. In fact, they were overbooked. There was no room for me. However, Mrs. Lee happened to have some pull, since she had built their music center! They made room for me. I completed four years and received a degree in Bible with a minor in Greek. Mrs. Lee paid for every cent of it. (May God remember her with great kindness.) I didn't play organized baseball ever again, but Coach Small and the York team went on to do well. However, I don't regret what I got in exchange -- my theological training, my first taste of missions, and my wife! Donna and I married after graduation and joined a mission team to work in rural East Africa.

It was during our time there that the third intervention by God occurred. Drought ravaged the region where we lived. For almost two years the rains failed, and I witnessed the incredible devastation. In a large scale natural disaster like drought, people starve, livestock dies, wildlife perishes, the economy shrivels, and illness increases. Then desperation enters as an entire nation's shoulders experience a collective slump. I also experienced the drain of the incessant heat, the dust, and the parched landscape, even as our fervent prayers ascended to God. The bottom line, however, was that across the nation, no rain was falling. Then I got a call from our sponsoring church in Cuyahoga Falls, Ohio. The missions committee chairman told me that the next week's entire Sunday service would be dedicated to prayer and petition for rain for Kenya. I thanked him. It was a good gesture and their prayers wouldn't hurt. On that special Sunday, nearing sunset in Kenya, the air was cooler and, well -- frisky. Crossing our yard from the small guest quarters toward the main house, I heard something hit the ground to my right. I heard it again, only someplace several feet away. Then something hit me. Raindrops! HUGE raindrops were striking around me. The atmosphere suddenly filled with the scent of rain! Could it be true? Dare I get my hopes up? Even before I could answer, I was running to my house through drops so large they stung! The drought had broken. I looked at my watch. Kenya is 7 hours ahead of Ohio. It was noon there and the special prayer service would have just concluded!

There have been other instances when I, or a group of us, prayed and witnessed our requests become reality, but these have especially impacted me. They have taught me that God hears and that He answers. Certainly, there were many times when prayer, fervent prayer, was offered, and yet what I requested was not granted. This used to bother me and caused me, for a time, to question if prayer worked, or more exactly if God worked. It also bothered me because the idea that prayer was merely a psychologically soothing exercise, or even worse, an empty ritual, was nauseating.

Unanswered prayer doesn't upset me as it once did. Now, I see it for what it is. I don't mean I see the unanswered prayer for what it is; I mean I see prayer for what it is. Prayer is talking with God, not dictating to Him what I want Him to do and then holding Him to some formulaic obligation. God is God. I'm a man, allowed to enter His presence. Privileged to speak with Him -- even welcomed to speak with Him -- I'm allowed to present my requests, but they are just that -- requests. My requests are little more than holding out my hand for assistance. I'm the beggar dependent upon the generosity and graciousness of my Lord and King.

God is God and in that position can do as He pleases. To my favor, He is a good God. He is also a wise God. Sitting above the circle of the universe, He sees all from start to finish, and from that vantage, considers in all matters the good of those who seek Him. If I take that to mean that He will work everything out to be what I'd like to happen in my life, I will sometimes be disappointed and question the effectiveness of prayer. However, if I know that God is above the "circle," and is good, and that, for the overall good of all of us who believe in Him, He will give what is best, then whether He gives what I ask or withholds it, I can accept His reply because I know it is the very best reply for me.

This insight has changed my feelings toward unanswered prayers. It removed the angst I felt when nothing happened. It evaporated the disappointment, anger, and confusion rising from my unmet (and unfounded) expectations of God. It let God be God and me be His honored guest and dearly beloved one. When we let God make the big decisions, we benefit, now or later, individually or collectively, from the wisdom and kindness of He who sits above the circle of the universe making perfect and loving judgments, always. God considers all our prayers. At times our requests move Him to action. Prayer, then, is a place of peace, calm, comfort, and safety in addition to one of power.

Leading up to 1987, these and other events prepared me for what would occur in that year during an unplanned, friendly visit to the home of missionary friends Steve and Pam Workman. After visiting all together for a short time, Steve and I stepped into his office. It was small and efficient, with walls completely hidden behind bookshelves. Among the hundreds of books, my eyes focused upon a single worn little red-jacketed volume. Why that particular book captured my attention is part of the mystery in this story. But that book would lead me, as Phantastes had Lewis, onto a wonderful and great frontier and raise the question, "Has this been an encounter with chance or Providence?" Its uninspiring title, *The Autobiography of George Müller*, drew my attention nonetheless, and I asked to borrow it. Müller's story was riveting. The privileged, rebellious, hedonistic advent of his life, culminating in a magnanimous, selfless conclusion that created a 150-year ripple effect on following generations set a fire in my heart and delivered me onto a new frontier.

Until age 24 Müller was a man-of-the-flesh. Ironically, his father, a successful businessman, had hoped for his son to secure a good position as a clergyman, but George would have none of it. That is, until God opened his eyes in a jail cell and redirected the course of his life. As his heart changed, so did his companions. Müller found a kindred spirit, colleague, and close personal friend in Mr. Craik. Together they experienced considerable success as preachers and evangelists, but it was a stepping stone in a greater and broader legacy. Müller went on to establish one of the largest orphanages in the world and 117 schools totaling 120,000 pupils. He would receive a presidential invitation to the United States White House, and, though living in very modest circumstances himself, would personally contribute today's equivalent of millions of dollars to Christian missions. According to Müller, all this served one greater legacy -- the provision of proof that God still hears and answers prayer.

Though admittedly callous before his conversion, Müller's heart became one of the most gentle and sensitive. He found it unsettling to proclaim a Gospel of love and yet turn a blind eye to the plight of orphaned and needy children living in the street outside his door. In response, he opened the doors of his own house to shelter and care for five street children. Though stretched financially and cramped for space, he and Mrs. Müller took additional children into their care, yet there were still children in need -- many, many, more. Müller prayed for God to help him and his wife meet the needs of those still suffering … and God did. With no appeal for assistance, bottles of milk appeared on the door stoop; clothing and bedding came from neighbors; small cash gifts were handed to the couple by strangers; and yet, more children remained in need.

Care for orphans became Müller's calling. He and his wife served the orphaned of England for the next 60 years with the conviction that if he would pray for their supplies, God would provide all that was necessary to meet the needs of His people. Not doubting that God would bring food, clothing, medicine, education, and spiritual training to the orphans under his care, his life became a megaphone heard literally around the world, heralding that God indeed

[Sketch of George Müller by Martha Provost]

still heard and answered prayer. Over the course of his 91 years, Müller housed, clothed, educated, fed, and provided for the medical and spiritual needs of over 10,000 children and as many as 200 staff members and their families. These accomplishments are even more eye-opening knowing that Müller never publicly nor privately solicited a single farthing from any person for the care of himself, his staff, or the orphans! He purposely kept secret the orphans' needs. Every need, no matter how large or small, was taken to God in the closet of prayer. There, earnest and humble petition

solicited the Hand of Grace to move hearts around the world to meet every need and concern.

DEER RUN (1989 - 1992)

In 1989, two years after reading Müller's story, our lives took an unexpected turn. My mother's failing health demanded more direct care. We tearfully withdrew from our beloved mission in Africa and returned to the US as the administrative directors of a summer youth camp and retreat facility in East Texas. Camp Deer Run had been my childhood summer Bible encampment. I knew first-hand the power of the ministry it had offered. Though the loss of our ministry in Kenya was terribly saddening to us, we embraced the invitation to Deer Run with enthusiasm -- naive about what lay ahead. The unraveling began immediately. Before we had driven away from DFW airport I received distressing news. Matters related to our employment at Camp Deer Run were changed. Chief among those changes involved my salary -- there was none! I have never inquired into the details of how that transpired, but the fact remained that those who had agreed to support me as camp director had changed their minds. Donna and I, of course, had not pursued other options in the six months leading up to our departure from Kenya. As a result, this sudden change in arrangements left us jobless and homeless with two small children. Our possessions consisted of what we carried in our suitcases and what we were wearing. Whether this change of events was chance or Providence we did not know; the only things that were certain were the lumps in our throats and the knots in our stomachs.

Many would have run away from the situation we found at Deer Run, and many counseled us that we should. And honestly, if not for Müller's story resonating in my mind, I'd have walked away from it myself. I don't think we'd have been judged by man or God if we had. The camp was physically in shambles -- 100 acres and 20 buildings with only a push mower and a crescent wrench as tools for their maintenance. Screened windows were ripped; doors were broken or missing. Electrical wiring was antiquated and dangerously exposed. The grounds were overgrown and littered, and the road running throughout the encampment was eroded. Ditches down the center were too deep for vehicles to cross. Roofs leaked; spoiled food sat in refrigerators and freezers; and the ancient septic pump leached into the creek. Rusted pipes led to water leaks costing $300 a month even when the camp was not in operation! To top it off, total monthly income and donations to the camp were only $240.00.

You may question, "Why didn't he check this out before signing on?" It's a good question. The truth is that I did inquire about many matters before accepting the job. I asked about debt and was told the camp had none. I asked about housing and was told it would be provided. I asked about income and had been assured that an area church would support us. I asked about the condition of the facilities and knew they were in need of repair. I also knew that enrollment was near zero. But, I was 9000 miles away. I trusted those who invited me.

As I explained, it was literally at the airport that I learned there was no funding for my position. I later learned that the camp was only receiving $240.00 per month for all its expenses. I had been told that the camp was debt free; but in the first few months after starting to work, I discovered there was almost $12,000 in debt. How these apparent misrepresentations could occur among Believers is a question I had but never investigated. Miscommunication happens even among the best-intended souls. Perhaps, I misunderstood what I heard. Perhaps, others misunderstood. Perhaps, expectations and hopes were prematurely presented as accomplished fact. How it happened doesn't matter because, as you will soon learn, God turned it into good for my family, the camp, the Kingdom, and me. What God does, especially among broken and failed people, is all that ever matters.

The physical and financial conditions of the encampment were bad, really bad, but the spiritual condition was even worse. Enrollment was down. Only 214 children had attended the entire summer before our arrival. Even twenty years earlier, when I'd been a camper, enrollment was nearer 700. As I learned, the director and staff ahead of me had left a dark legacy spiritually. All but two local churches had withdrawn their involvement, and even those two were tenuous. In fact, on the third day at my new job, one of those churches informed me that they were dropping their support. Only the Church of Christ in Winnsboro, Texas stayed behind us with $200.00 per month. Who then, in their right mind, would have taken on such a fiasco? No one. But we weren't thinking like everyone else; we were thinking like George Müller, and we believed in a God who had used the camp powerfully for decades. We believed He could do it again.

Clinging to Müller's example, Donna and I stopped our minivan in the wooded cathedral of sweet gum and pine outside the gate of the camp. Our young sons, napping in their car seats, were awakening with excitement. It had been a very demanding and draining six months since my mother's phone call. It was a sobering moment for Donna and me. We were stepping into that "great frontier" C. S. Lewis had written of. I put the transmission in park and turned off the engine. The sounds of Deer Run filled the void. With my family in agreement, I then offered an audible declaration to the LORD:

"O LORD,

We are here. You have brought us to this place. It seems to have been You who planned and ordered and designed our being here today. Thank You.

Lord of All, this is Your ground. We are Your servants. Bring honor to Your Name. Work Your plans. Accomplish Your goals. Use us as You see fit. It is more than we can accomplish, but we know it is a simple thing to You. Resurrect, grow, expand this camp and the ministry it provides in the lives of children and adults. Broaden Your Kingdom from this place.

Lord, we are not sure of this, but our hearts urge us to seek Your face in prayer for all the provisions of the camp. We are willing to trust You for everything needed for this ministry. We will trust You for financial provisions. We will trust You for helpers. We will trust You for our needs. We will trust You for godly staff. We will trust You to bring the children. We will trust You to nudge your people to supply every need. We will tell what You have done. The testimony of Your work here will be the greatest gift we will leave here. May those who are blessed by this ministry hear of Your work in answer to prayer alone and may their own faith be built up. May the world know that You are and that You still respond to the petitions of people.

Oh, God. We trust You. You have never failed us yet. Our lives are in Your hands. Thank You for calling us to this work. We are honored. May Your Name be exalted.

According to the Will of the Savior, let all these things be done. Amen."

It was admittedly subjective, but Donna and I had concluded that our chief work through the camp was allowing God the opportunity to prove His readiness to hear and answer prayer. By trusting Him with the camp as Müller had his orphanages. Donna was in agreement and committed to pray, work, and wait for God to nudge people to supply needed funds and materials and manpower. It was frightening, yet also deeply inspiring, as over and over again God rose to the occasion, restoring the camp's grounds and buildings, increasing enrollment, eliminating all debt, and supplying our salary. Though we have never had any qualms with fund-raising through direct appeal, during those years it was only in the closet of prayer that we expressed our needs to God. Each answer to our prayers was a pebble of evidence. Taken individually they might be shrugged off as coincidence, but collectively they are weighty evidence that God still hears and answers prayer. A few of those many prayer answers have become especially meaningful to me, and I hope they will be for you too.

As our prayers ramped up, our challenges avalanched. The tiny camp office was in chaos. Stacks of papers, as high as three and four feet, rested against the walls, on the floor, and on the desk. There was no staff to help me sort through and file it. Being more of an idea person and not much on detail, that mountain of paper was an Everest to me. I was mentally paralyzed at the prospect of working through it; in fact, I literally had no idea where to begin. So, I put two things on my prayer list: a computer and a secretary.

About two weeks after arriving at Deer Run, the full extent of its physical brokenness began to surface. The plumbing and the electrical wiring needed repair and replacement. The grounds were eroding, overgrown, and littered. Roofs leaked, windows were missing, structures were falling, and fences were down. There were a few things I knew I could repair and some I could learn how to repair, but the sheer amount of need was more than I could manage. I needed a handyman. "Lord, send us someone who knows how to repair all of this… and we don't have any tools. So, send us a repairman and send us tools." This became part of my daily prayer.

[CDR open septic tank]

One of our first days there, I noticed a septic cover was missing near one of the boy's bathhouses. The septic tank was totally exposed! Any child could have walked out of the bathhouse at night and fallen into it. This had to be repaired ASAP. So, I added a septic cover on my prayer list. Yes, I actually asked God for a cement lid to cover our toilet waste.

The hazard presented by the septic situation called for prompt action. I called a former director and asked where I might find a new cover. He told me the name of the company that had installed it. I drove to their location about 45 minutes away. Introducing myself, I gave them the dimensions of the septic system opening. Noticing I didn't have a truck, the clerk asked how I would carry it. Almost four feet across and several inches thick, the concrete and wire-mesh top must have weighed over 200 pounds! I had prepared for carrying the lid home by removing the center and rear seats from my van. I explained this to clarify how I would carry it back in the van. The guy smirked. In East Texas that either means, "What a nut!" or it means, "Bless this poor guy's heart." Two ways of saying the same thing.

Now, at this point, there was absolutely no money in the camp account. Donna and I, however, had decided to use $10,000.00 of our personal funds as 'startup funds.' Until He began to supply us or the $10,000.00 ran out, we told the Lord that we'd put that money to use for our personal needs, utilities, fuel, or the needs of the camp. I reasoned if God were truly behind this effort, He would move others to help, and if He were not behind it, it would not prosper. He would not forget our faithfulness. We had nothing to lose. Still, every penny was pinched hard. "You say this is for that camp?" the clerk asked as we slammed the hatch shut on my now squatting minivan. "Yes. We've just started working there and hope to have a full house next summer," I replied. "Well, tell you what. Just take that cover with you. No charge. It's our donation," he said. I was totally prepared and had expected to pay for the lid. So, there was not hint of financial need. By all appearances, we were able to pay. This was the first clear instance of God nudging a person to donate a specifically requested item of need to the camp.

A couple of days later the phone in our tiny camp office rang. Scrambling in search, I discovered it buried under a pile of papers on the desk. A Christian brother from Tyler, about 30 miles away, heard we had come on board. He, like we, had a heart for this particular ministry to children. As he spoke the pounding in my ears grew so loud I could hardly hear him. "I have a little computer shop over here in Tyler. Do you have any computer needs? I figure I can get you something if you need it." My heart raced, but I tried to remain calm, not sure if he was donating a computer or selling one. "Yes, we've been thinking that we need one here in the office." I waited to hear if this was a sales pitch or another nudge by God. "I figure I can get you one over there maybe next week. It'll be used, but will probably serve you all well until you can get something else later. I'll be happy to give it to the camp. I could even deliver it if that helps." I'm certain he had no idea just how much his gift helped us, or the retelling of the account would help inspire others decades later.

Still, Deer Run had many needs, among them, mattresses. The ones on the cabin bunks must have been from the Civil War era. Not really, but I was told they had been purchased from an army surplus supply 20 or more years ago. Their cotton stuffing had absorbed East Texas humidity and 10-year-old nighttime mishaps far too long -- moms were unwilling to place their cherubs on those filthy mats. After a good examination, we decided 50 were usable, but 100 others absolutely had to be replaced. "Lord, we need 100 new mattresses before camp starts next summer." Like Cortés at Veracruz, we burned our ships behind us. In faith (and out of love for those moms), we hauled 100 old mattresses to the dump.

One morning, while standing on our porch in the center of camp, I heard the sound of a vehicle entering the gates. Now, Deer Run is literally at the end of a country road. Beyond it is a swamp. So, when a vehicle passes through the camp's gates it is either lost or destined for camp. The rusting dull red Ford truck squeaking and popping its way into camp, gave no clues as to which this visit might be. I greeted the wrinkled, Santa Clause-like, elderly gentleman in overalls who stepped from the cab. He began: "Hello. My name's Griffith and I live just up the road. Heard you're here trying to start up the camp again." "Yes, sir," I affirmed. "My name is Steve. Good to meet you." After a bit of chit-chat, Mr. Griffith, in a genuine and genteel way, said, "Well, Steve, me and the wife's retired now so if you can use it, we'd like to offer to help out around here. I'm no expert (he actually was), but I know a little about most anything associated with plumbing, carpentry, electric and such. The wife -- she knows a good bit about crafts. I have most of the tools a man might need. I live just up the hill. I could be here about any time you needed me."

Of course, I accepted with enthusiasm and gratitude. He set to work on our water problems that same afternoon. Within a week, every water leak had been repaired! Several months later, we were delighted to be able to offer Mr. Griffith a few dollars an hour for his work, which he reluctantly accepted.

The immediate grounds and ball fields amounted to about five acres. Our only lawn care tool was a small push mower until in the early spring when a gentleman unloaded a tractor and bush hog in my drive. "Use it till I come get it," he said. We used it the entire time we were at camp. I don't know if he ever came back to get it.

Through the fall, winter, and spring I ran a busy campaign visiting churches and youth groups, promoting summer camps. My promise was to restore the spiritual integrity of the camp and provide a safe and clean environment for children. The response of churches, parents, and children was enthusiastic and encouraging, raising our hopes.

One of those evenings, with a group after church services, hot dogs, chips, dips, etc. were being served. As things wound down and we were helping with the cleanup, Donna noticed how much food was being left over -- it was a lot. In Africa, we'd seen too much poverty to waste food ever again. As well, though we were pinching every penny to stretch the $10,000, it was getting thin. While she washed dishes, Donna secretly asked the Lord to move the kitchen helpers to offer us the leftovers. Then, just before tossing everything in the waste can, one of the ladies paused, turned to Donna and asked, "Could you use these leftovers?" We could not have been more grateful for God moving at that moment.

I love cattle and have lots of experience with them, but I am very uncomfortable around horses, and I think they know it. As can be imagined, the camp facility had needs on many levels, and some were unique. Deer Run, for example, had operated a trail riding element for years, and campers had come to expect it. Typically, the horses were farmed out to individuals for care during the winter and then returned to camp for the summer months. However, this year we had a problem -- a big one -- we had no corrals.

The barbed wire, t-posts, and rusted gates that had served as fencing for many years were in shambles. It was clear that this tangle was dangerous to horses and children, and if we were to provide trail riding this year, we must replace the existing corrals. I was NOT qualified to tackle that task, but I could pray for someone who could. "Lord, if You want this for the children, then we'll need materials for corrals and someone to build them."

This is the story, taken from one of my journal entries, of how God responded to my requests:

"George Müller asked the Lord to provide even the most humble items necessary for the care of the children in his trust. Perhaps the story of God's timely provision for our equestrian program is an example of just how involved with us He really is.

The first day I walked up the hill behind our trailer to the old corrals I found a ghost town of defunct wire, pipe, and mesh panels. A coyote slipped into the forest as I turned to my left and wasps dove in and out of the barn near me. It was desolate on "Horse Hill." Immediately, it became clear to me that everything would have to be replaced. Otherwise, there could be no horse program at Camp Deer Run. That would leave a lot of children disappointed, and perhaps they would interpret it as a sign of weakness on God's part. October had crept in on us already.

I put the corrals near the top of my prayer list. Now, I am not particularly fond of horses -- they scare me -- but a lady who lives about 8 miles from camp loves them. Stacy had been a camp volunteer there before I came and had been involved with the horse program especially. One day she came to the camp and agreed with me that the whole area needed to be leveled and rebuilt. She said, "If you get some pipe, my husband and some other fellows will build the corrals." That was the first sign which suggested that the Lord would provide for the new pens.

I asked Stacy if she and her husband, David, would draw up some plans for the corrals and then tell me how much pipe and other supplies they would need. They did and within a couple of weeks I was praying for 30 lengths of pipe and enough cement, paint, and sucker rod to complete the job. I knew that at one time oil companies in the area gave used pipe away. I prayed that we'd be given the pipe or the money. Secretly, I suspected that some oil company would give us the pipe. This was now November.

I prayed almost every day for these items. During this time I kept the need to myself. When someone asked about the horse program I just told them that we were planning to build new corrals and would have the program if we completed them in time. In the meantime, two other welders offered their services when we got the materials.

Mr. Griffin and I tore down the old corrals. It was a tough decision. I could have patched the old ones and perhaps made it through one more summer, but it would have also been to admit that we did not believe that God would provide. So, we started pulling old fence posts and wrapping up old wire. Still, no pipe. It was now March!

Shortly after we pulled the fences down, a friend approached me one evening after church service and asked how things were at camp. I gave a report of the many positives we were experiencing. He said, "Steve, if there is anything I can do for you, you let me know." I felt it was an open door that I should reply to with honesty. I told him that I did have one need that perhaps he could help me with, since he worked in the oil industry. "I need about 30 lengths of pipe," I said. He replied, "Well, I don't know if I can get any or not these days. The companies used to give that stuff away, but they will hardly do it anymore." I don't think it was obvious, but my heart sank a little. However, he promised to check in a couple of places.

Another three weeks passed and he never mentioned it again, though we saw each other regularly at church. I assumed he either had forgotten or had not found anything. At any rate, I did not want to interfere, only trust in The Provider. I waited. Six weeks remained until camp would open.

One late April evening, he and I were together and he said, "Hey, Steve. I have checked all over the place for some pipe and nobody has anything they'll give us, but I have one more place I'll see this week." I thought, "Ok Lord, I'll ride it on out to the wire."

I think it was on a Thursday that I drove into camp and Donna told me, "Look up on the hill." There it was -- piles of pipe! I later learned that he had not been given the pipe from the company he had asked as a last resort, but from another one that he happened to visit on his way home one evening. During their conversation, the pipe came up and the owner not only gave him the 30 lengths we requested but added another 10! Even more, he loaned his company truck and trailer to deliver it to camp!

The welders began immediately. Ten days before opening day at camp a small pen was finished and serious progress was being made on three larger ones. Then, we hit a snag. There would not be enough pipe and we had no sucker rod or paint. I had continued to pray all along, and to be honest, I was ready for this one to be over, but *still we needed these items. I asked how much was still needed and the approximate cost. "It'll take about $700 to complete the job," David told me. I gulped. Camp did not have $700. "Perhaps the Lord wants me to give of my own supplies," I thought. So, I called a company and ordered the remaining supplies. They delivered them the following day and construction continued. It appeared we'd make the deadline, but this would not be the end of the story.*

The Saturday before camp was to open on Sunday, some friends of camp were on the property cleaning the grounds, when one of them turned to me abruptly and asked, "Who paid for that extra pipe?" I told him, "I did." He shot back, "You call Clark S. and tell him that his cousin Jay told him that you needed $700." I went straight to the phone and dialed.

"Hello Mr. S., this is Steve Meeks from Camp Deer Run and I have been given a message that may seem a little awkward. Your cousin Jay has been at camp today and he suggested that I tell you of a need we have in regards to the building of our horse corrals."

He interrupted, "How much do you need, Steve?"

"Seven hundred dollars."

"Ok, I'll get you a check right away."

The welders worked all that Saturday. As evening closed, the final weld was completed as Stacy, her kids, and our wrangler placed the finishing touches of paint on the last corral. That night our horses rested in their new quarters. God had done it and we still had eighteen hours left before camp opened."

Camp facilities received a dramatic facelift during the three months prior to our first summer. Kitchen and bathhouses were thoroughly cleaned. The cabins, once a collage of various whites, grays, and reds over the years, were repainted in an alpine red and pine-forest green scheme. The pool pump had been repaired as well as the septic system pump house. The camp's entire wiring system was upgraded to meet code. Ceiling fans now cooled every cabin (we had no A/C), and the plumbing was repaired throughout. Still, with only two weeks left before the first campers were to arrive, acres of brushy overgrowth covered ball fields and cabin areas, trash and debris littered the grounds, and the road remained impassable. 50 of the 100 mattresses we had been praying for had been supplied through donations, but we needed 50 more, and we needed ten more ceiling fans -- six for the dining hall and four for the rec hall. A friend of camp spoke to a ceiling fan manufacturer about our need. The manufacturer was willing to sell us ceiling fans at a discount -- $50 each.

I prayed daily about these matters, trying not to panic. Monday morning, I checked the mail to discover a letter from the Browns in Gilmer, Texas that contained a check for $300 and a handwritten note, "Use this for ceiling fans." So, the Brown's gift was exactly enough to buy six! Of course, this was very encouraging, but God intended to answer the prayer completely. A year later, the Browns sent an additional gift. What I wrote them included a postscript. In the postscript, I wrote an update on how God used them to answer our specific prayer request for ceiling fans.

"PS... I think I mentioned how your first gift for the ceiling fans was a direct answer to a prayer offered for those items. By the way, we have purchased the fans. Your money went farther than we had expected. God used two other servants in the Kingdom to get us new, 5-speed, commercial fans at only $30.00 each!! That means your money was enough to place fans in the dining hall (6) and the rec hall (4). Isn't God exciting?!"

Never, during the next three years of my time as camp director, did the camp receive the offer of another ceiling fan. God provided exactly what we requested and exactly what we needed.

An area-wide 'Deer Run Work Day' had become a tradition among many of the churches in East Texas in which families descended on the camp one Saturday in the spring and conducted a sweeping cleanup of the grounds. This tradition had grown up during the many years I was away from camp, so when someone suggested I organize one, I did. However, there was a problem.

I learned about it late in the spring, and there was only one Saturday that we could have it. This meant we had only a single shot at a total camp cleanup. With 20 building and 100 acres, that's a lot to do in about eight hours. The only weekend available was the one before the opening of camp.

Clouds gathered throughout the Friday afternoon before the scheduled workday, and that night it rained; actually, it poured. Early Saturday morning I was awake, praying and worrying. Clouds hung low. Skies were gray, the ground soaked, and my heart sinking. "We can't drive tractors on this soggy ground, and the lightning is too dangerous. Lord, we need a hand here."

About 7:30 a.m. a lone pickup quietly crept into the camp and parked. David Bradbury, one of my childhood mentors, emerged. He'd driven almost an hour on his day off, in dreary conditions. With his arrival, the day did seem to brighten. He pulled a chainsaw and a pair of gloves from the truck's cab as I walked toward him to offer a welcome, but before we got through our handshake a second vehicle lumbered in pulling a trailer with a tractor on board. Vehicle after vehicle streamed through the gates carrying men, boys, and their families. Parking became congested, in fact. Weed eaters, lawn mowers, leaf blowers, tractors, hand tools, gloves and goggles, mops and brooms, even a flamethrower and a bulldozer arrived. I could not believe it! And if this were not enough, the sun broke through. By 9 a.m. the sky was clear and the ground had completely dried! Literally, the sandy soil at camp had drained like a clean pipe. It even supported the dozer. The sounds of machinery and happy chatter had camp buzzing like a hive of bees -- sweet music to Donna and me.

That evening, back to the chirp of crickets and birds, standing with a few of the last remaining volunteers in a spotlessly clean campground, I fielded questions about how camp was going. West Soward was one of those half-dozen men standing with me at the dining hall. Leaning against a tree, his question startled me, "Hey, how many more mattresses do you need?" I paused. We hadn't been talking about mattresses. I hadn't told anyone we still needed mattresses. In a split second, a silent conversation took place in my mind, "This could be one of those moments when God would place a pebble in my bag. What was I to do? Tell him? Wait and let God nudge him?" I didn't know, so I hesitated. Then, he continued, "How about 50?" I could not believe it. Exactly what we needed. "Yes. 50 would be great," I replied. "Okay, order them and have the bill sent to my office," he said. I did, and they were delivered the Friday before camp opened on Sunday. Exactly 100 new mattresses had been donated and without a mention of our need for them. How did West even know? It's all pretty amazing enough, but there is more. In the course of our next three years at camp, no one ever offered to buy mattress number 101.

[CDR clean up day group]

[Old mattresses]

[New mattresses]

My college staff and I navigated an exhausting week of training and preparation between the close of that fabulous area-wide workday and the opening day of camp. It was now Sunday afternoon, and everyone was in position to receive our first campers. The grounds were immaculate and the buildings repaired and painted with new mattresses on our bunks. Just after noon, the first nervous parents and excited cherubs arrived through the camp gate. I had recruited a good staff for this first year, but most had never attended Deer Run as children. Over the week, I'd done my best to load into them all the camp traditions, songs, and camp lore that I could. They probably were overloaded and I was exhausted, but camp was at last open! Everything ran like a top -- for about two minutes, *literally* two minutes.

I'd developed a plan for receiving and registering campers that kept cars off the grassy areas (where the water and septic pipes were buried), kids safe, and parents informed at all times. I don't think Disneyland could have done better. The staff warmly greeted families and welcomed with enthusiasm. Registration formalities took only about five minutes. Non-counseling staff grabbed armloads of camper 'necessities' and escorted kids and parents to the cabins. Counselors then met their campers, introduced themselves to the parents, and helped settle campers into their bunks. As this finely tuned system was humming along, my plan was to leisurely mingle with the parents as I sipped ice tea beneath palm trees soaked in butter-balm suntan lotion (okay, I'm exaggerating). It actually was my plan to receive guests and be available at registration to handle any special needs or registration queries. On my way to the registration area, I never made it to the registration tables. One of the girl staff yelled from across the camp, "Mr. Meeeeeeks! You need to come over here." Arrggghh! I knew it was some sort of a problem. I hoped only a minor one.

"I think there is something wrong," she explained. She was right.

It seems a truism that what can go wrong will go wrong at the worst time. So, in the first minutes of the opening day, with over 250 people on our grounds -- about 60% of them females -- the bathhouse plumbing blew up. The girl staff member had discovered that a very foul-smelling pool had formed just outside the door of the girl's bathhouse. I asked her to find Mr. Griffin and ask him to bring a shovel. She delayed and I then remembered it was just after noon on Sunday. Mr. Griffin might not have made it back from church and lunch yet. I was right. Because it was urgent, I needed the repair done as quickly as possible. I found a shovel and 'dug in' myself.

The sense of having qualified helpers covering the bases had been satisfying during those first few minutes; and it had felt nice to be clean and not sweating. (If you've lived in East Texas in the summer, you know what I mean.) But it was not to last. I was dripping in sweat within minutes. The sewer had not been on my agenda, but my responsibility and Kingdom responsibilities, I was learning, are sometimes quite lowly jobs.

There were two other memorable occasions when I felt sorry for myself during those Deer Run years. One came the year after the opening day, but the first was six months before the septic system backup, on our first Christmas day at camp. In six months, we had closed our ministry in Africa, moved across the world, and begun to turn the tide at camp. It had been a non-stop full-throttle time, and this Christmas morning, I decided, would be a day I would not work or even think about camp. I had in mind to take a leisurely stroll across the grounds simply to enjoy the beauty of the place and the scent of forest, and to experience the crispy morning air. Out the door and down the steps of our trailer I strode, taking in a deep long breath. East Texas winters aren't usually cold until late January or February, but it was a bit brisk that morning.

In an hour or so, I felt the tension in my shoulders relax. A satisfied smile lit my face and for about 100 steps I was enjoying what I had set out to experience. Then, my foot sunk into the ground several inches and I heard a sloshing noise. "What? Oh no! No! No! Nooooooo!" I moaned aloud. I was angry. I was disgusted. I was disheartened. Mr. Griffin had repaired so many leaks, but we must have missed one. "Here I am, Lord. I left what I loved in Africa! I've endured a lot and done my best. I've offered my money and time. Donna and I have gone without comforts and given up a lot. Why do I have to do this today? Of all days… why today?" I admit, I felt sorry for myself.

As soon as I said the words aloud, I heard myself and knew I was wrong. I repented because, of all days, this was *the* day. It was the day (at least the one we recognize) when the King had given up everything, offered His best, and traveled far for us -- for me. I stopped my complaining and found a shovel. It was a good day. It was a beautiful place. The air was still cool and clean. I was healthy enough to dig out around the pipe and repair the leak. The kids would still pull the paper wrapping from their gifts. In that moment, I realized I had just unwrapped my gift from its wet, soggy wrapping. His love and concern for me had newer, deeper, more personal meaning than six months earlier or even the night before. My sacrifices were nothing; He gave everything, so great was His love for me -- for us.

The second time I hosted a personal "poor-me" session was a few weeks before camp opened the second season. Things were much smoother and I'd grown accustomed to Mr. Griffin handling plumbing needs, but sure enough, with a spring retreat group at camp, a toilet in the girl's bathhouse (Hmmm, seems those girls were hard on that place…) sprang a leak. Grabbing a few hand tools and a replacement water line that went from the floor to the back of the tank, I set to repairing it myself. Now, unscrewing the line where it connects to the tank requires leaning over the bowl. If you can envision my posture, you'll understand that when I refocused my eyes from the pipe fitting to the toilet seat, I suddenly realized that something like two inches separated my cheeks from where someone else's had been! A disgusting image, isn't it?

Instantly, I drew back. Repulsed, I stood with my hands on my hips and declared to myself, "I have a college degree. I speak three languages. In fact, I'm one of only about seven Westerners in the entire world to speak one of them! I know how to live internationally. I can speak publicly, I write, I…," and I don't recall what more I listed, but it was quite an impressive compilation of all the things qualifying me for more than sticking my face against a toilet seat! Then, as during the previous Christmas, I caught myself. I laughed, "Got me again." Again, I repented, picked up my tools, and finished the job. With that, the toilet was repaired, and so was I.

On a more complimentary note, I was looking back through my Deer Run files and discovered a list of prayer answers containing 89 specific answers received between the donation of that computer in October of 1989 and a $100 gift by David Allen in February of 1991. These weren't all the donations or gifts given during that time, but some I felt I should record in giving glory to God. The specific items are diverse. They include cash gifts given to us personally, gifts to the camp ranging between $10.00 and $4300.00, free dental and medical treatment, weed eaters, five gallons of gasoline, furniture, equipment for the camp kitchen, a ping-pong table, an electrical pole, and flowers that were planted at the camp entrance. All these were answers to specific requests and they were made when people obeyed the nudge of God on their hearts -- none came as a result of our campaigning or asking. One item on that list stands apart from the others. It came as the second summer of camp drew to a close. The first summer had gone so well that camp numbers swelled. Each session grew exponentially over the previous. If the trend continued, we'd need more staff our second year. In the spring of 1991, before recruiting that year's college staff, I approached my board of directors about a pay raise for my summer workers. For years camp had been paying them only $40 a week; I felt we should do more and the trend in enrollment indicated the increase would be sustainable. The board allowed me to increase salaries by 150% to $100 a week, which wasn't a huge wage; but given that we personally still had not been fully paid for our work of the past 18 months, it was a true stretch of faith.

The third week in the summer I realized we were not going to reach my enrollment projections. I estimated a financial shortfall of $6500.00 and knew I had two choices: cut costs by sending some staff home or pray for God to make up the difference. The easier of the two was to let a few of the staff take a couple of weeks off and then come back in sessions that were almost full. It was easier, but it was not ethical. My staff had forgone more lucrative jobs to be at Deer Run. Their purpose was not financial; it was spiritual. They had come to serve kids in Jesus' name. Sending them home might make financial sense, but it was disloyal. So option number two became my only real choice. I took it.

I called three of the men's staff aside. "Guys, we need to pray. Get a sleeping bag and some water. We're going to fast and pray for three days." I don't recall asking if they would join me; I just told them, but they never balked. This was in the days before cell phones. We were going to the far corner of Deer Run property and could only be reached by messenger. So I left instructions with my program director about our location along with strict instructions to contact me only in the event of an emergency. We were going to meet with God, and I wanted our full attention available for Him. Those three long days in the heat, feeding the mosquitoes and ticks of East Texas, are a bit of blur now, over twenty-five years later. I don't remember the specifics of our conversations or prayers other than the general pattern we followed, rotating between prayer, reading Scripture, brief chats, and sleeping. The lack of food and the humid heat, combined with our physical exhaustion from the first three weeks of camp, drained us quickly. We found ourselves napping through the day, waking at scheduled prayer times, dripping with sweat. A messenger was sent to us on our third day, but the 'emergency' was addressed without returning to camp and it did not upset our solitude. The final hour of those days remains the clearest to me. The guys and I prayed together one last time; petitioning God to send more campers or send the $6500.00 cash needed to meet all the summer staff salaries. We prayed one final time and packed up our gear, and then I sent them back to camp without me. I wanted a little more time to be alone with the LORD. Without the guys knowing it, I'd been privately adding a prayer to our corporate list. It was an item I simply felt 'nudged' to add, "Lord, when you supply us, do it in such a way as to build the faith of my staff."

So I stayed an extra half-hour with Him and then walked back to camp myself. On the way, I checked the mailbox, but the mail had already been taken to the office. On the way to the office, I stopped by the kitchen and grabbed a light snack. The secretary was in the office, but she had not received any additional enrollments or donations since we had left. "No problem," I thought, "maybe tomorrow." It was Wednesday. That week closed on Friday with no changes. I remained positive and expectant; however, nothing changed for the next two weeks. Then, with two weeks left in the summer, a married couple on the staff approached me. "Steve," Jeff started, "Brenda and I want you to keep our salaries for this session." I objected, but they insisted. They were in leadership positions, so their salaries were larger, totaling $500. That left a need of $6000.00.

The first day of the last session opened without even a single additional enrollment. The summer had gone much smoother than our first, and the old Deer Run atmosphere was back, with most of the staff being former Deer Run campers themselves. The schedule at Camp Deer Run (CDR) is almost as old as the camp -- hardly changing over four decades. Tradition is strong, and the final night of a two-week session must include a 'Camper vs. Staff' softball game followed by a quick dip in the pool, an awards time, and an especially meaningful night devotional.

The next morning campers are served their breakfast before parents swoop in to discover that their children have survived without them -- albeit with a few extra mosquito bites and scratches, not to mention a pile of really, really dirty clothes. The staff and I would meet at six a.m. and then again in the early afternoon when they had cleaned their area of work and said goodbyes to one another and were ready to pick up their final paycheck.

Knowing what lay ahead, I had instructed our accountant earlier in the week to write everyone his or her paycheck. The other vendors would expect payment the following week or by the end of the month, but perhaps a gift would come in over the weekend and we'd be able to pay all those debts too. But going into that final day, there was not enough in the account to do it all. I decided to trust the Lord. If worst came to worst, they could take me to jail or close the camp. I had done all I knew to do. It was out of my hands, and I was at peace. God would have to sort it out.

With the sun setting, but still enough light to see, the last out was made in the ball game as the 'Mighty Deer Run Staff' trounced the campers. (As always. Well, almost always.) Everyone made a mad dash to the pool where silly boys and male staff still in their jeans jumped, flipped, and flopped into the pool (This impressed the girls very much. Ha!). Anyway, as usual, gloves, balls, bats, and bases were strewn everywhere. Ever attentive to the camp's appearance, I began cleaning up. With my arms full of softball equipment, I was approached by an elderly visitor we'll name "Mr. C."

"Hey Steve," Mr. C. greeted me, "how's the summer gone?" I told him it had been wonderful, which it had been. He then asked, "Do you have a pocket?" I looked at my shirt pocket. He reached over and tucked a folded check in it. "You've done a good job. Hope that'll help," he said. I'd like to be able to say that I proceeded with great restraint and took the very high ground of not even considering how much that check was for, but I'd be dishonest. As soon as he disappeared from view, I unloaded the sports gear and peeked.

The next morning the staff gathered in the crafts hall for our daily staff briefing, which typically included special instructions for the day and a quick thought or devotion. This morning being the last one, everyone was feeling relieved and a bit more chipper than normal. On this morning, after adding a word of congratulations for a beautifully done job over the summer, I then read the passage in the Gospels where Jesus spoke to a stormy sea, "Peace, be still!" The Scripture says that it grew still immediately and His followers were astonished.

"You all know this has been a great but challenging summer. You've done a super job, and I'm proud of each of you. What a blessing to have been with you. You also have been praying with me about the financial situation. Thank you. We've all hoped for God to step in and relieve that strain with more campers or with a financial donation. We did receive a portion of the need, but still, $6000.00 remains outstanding. Well, I want you to know the LORD has spoken, 'Peace, be still!'" And with that, I held up the check Mr. C. had put into my pocket. It was for exactly $6000.00! The staff leaped to their feet, swapping high-fives and cheering. There were shouts, laughter, and tears. It was an inspiring moment for us all. God had answered not only all *our* prayers, but also all *my* prayers. Had the gift arrived earlier, it would have lost its impact. Had it arrived a day later, the staff would have already left. But by arriving at the final hour, it had been *in such a way as to increase the faith of my staff*. Surely, we serve a mighty God!

We loved the 1991 Deer Run staff. They were truly a delight to Donna and me. Still, more than 25 years later, we are friends and in occasional contact with many of them. In fact, only a few weeks ago I spoke with those three young men who prayed and fasted with me. They all quickly pointed to those three days as a spiritual high point in their lives. One of them now serves on the Deer Run Board of Directors. His family recently donated $200,000.00 to the camp to construct a new facility. I chuckle at the irony -- it is for a new dining room. At the same time, I marvel at how the seeds of faith, sown that summer, have grown, producing trust in God not money, the willingness to sacrifice for His purposes, and the fruit of generosity.

[CDR check for 6k]

Six months after that momentous day in August, I received a letter from the church where Mr. C. attended. One of their ministers wrote,

"Dear Steve,

...Here is your official notification that CDR is in the 1992 budget for $6000 ($500 a month). So the checks should keep coming! The congregation is very supportive of your work and pleased to be a part. We hope that this support draws you closer to your monthly goal. A big part of your "Thank You" goes to Mr. C. He really was the encourager for the support. He probably would be upset if he knew that I told you that."

I have since learned that this annual gift of $6000.00 continued for up to a decade after we left CDR.

When I first began to rebuild the camp, I had written a lengthy letter to area congregations. In it, I had said, "The key to Deer Run's success will be prayer. I am convinced that the degree to which we affect lives and reach into the world will be directly proportional to the hours that area congregations and members spend in prayer for her success. Prayer shall be the battle cry for Camp Deer Run in the 90's. We desire nothing short of Divine empowering of our ministry."

Interestingly, a niece and several of her friends came to our home in Tennessee for a spring break getaway in 2016. One of them wore a CDR t-shirt. She was dating an outstanding Christian young man who had grown up attending and later working on the staff at Camp Deer Run. I don't know this young man, but I feel that we had some part in his spiritual formation. Occasionally, by accident usually, we've run into those who have had their lives changed or shaped by a summer at Deer Run. As we supposed, many have served or are serving literally around the world.

Now, backing up to the late summer of 1990, after the completion of our first summer directing the camp, Donna and I both felt a tug back to Africa. It had come while attending a conference on missions in Abilene, Texas, and we talked about it on our five-hour drive home. Mom's condition was improving and the camp was on its feet, but a return to Africa faced hurdles -- big ones... impossible ones. We listed eleven things that must happen for us to return to Kenya. Of the eleven items, not one of them seemed possible; several would be considered ridiculous considering we covenanted not to mention them to anyone. Our silence guaranteed that no one would suspect we had any hope for returning to Africa again. If any one of these occurred, it would be due to the work of God and not us. If all eleven happened, it would be very weighty evidence of God's involvement.

The eleven impossible items were:

1. My brother needed to marry. We felt another woman in the family was needed to assist Mom and encourage her. Danny, my brother, was 30. He was not dating. It was a long-long-shot. (No offense little brother, but hey, just sayin'.)

2. Someone would need to ask for my job. This was crazy but necessary.

The board of directors was pleased with my work. No one wanted me gone. It was insane to imagine that someone would apply for my job since I would not reveal that I was considering something different. The notion would have to come from above.

3. The new director would have to be a former Deer Runner. The program at CDR is so unique that it wouldn't be operated in true Deer Run spirit with anyone but a former camper or staff member. This obviously limited our field considerably.

4. The new director had to have a missionary heart. We'd begun to move Deer Run in a missional direction, and we did not want that emphasis compromised. My replacement would need to be more than favorable about missions -- he would have to be driven by it.

5. A new director's house was mandatory. The manufactured home we lived in was falling apart. The ends sagged, the floor had two places where we could not step without running our leg through, and the toilet had already fallen through (really!) once. No one but us would put up with such an arrangement. Any new director and the board would have to craft a plan to provide him better housing, but the camp did not have the money. In fact, they were still in arrears to us for almost one year's salary.

6. Additional land would have to be purchased. We needed more property for the director's house because there was not space for additional housing on existing property. The camp's property on three sides was inadequate for a house, and the fourth side was fully utilized. The fifteen acres abutting the camp's entrance were perfect and for sale, but there was no money to purchase it and my policy was to not solicit people, only God. So we asked God for that piece of land.

7. A church would have to initiate any conversation with us regarding a return to Africa. How could anyone know our desires unless we told them? Clearly, no one can read minds, But though it seemed contrary to reason, we were convinced that we should not reveal our hope for a return. If God nudged someone to open the discussion, we would respond, but only as the doors opened ahead of us. Silence, prayer, and watching were our only actions.

8. One church should supply our personal oversight and financial support. More than a dozen churches and another dozen individuals supported our first years of service in Kenya. When reporting on furloughs the majority of our time involved traveling. A single sponsoring congregation would be a must to allow us more time to invest in my mother and Donna's parents when in the States. A separate fund, which we called "Work Fund," for fuel, airfare, printing, etc., could be from multiple sources, but ideally only a few, and near our primary sponsor.

9. Mom's health must improve to the point where she could live alone. The doctors could not treat or cure my mother's debilitating chronic pain. In fact, they could not agree on the root of the problem. Thus, we could not travel across the globe unless she were able to function on her own. Another impossibility, it seemed.

10. Mom would have to not only allow us to return, but *encourage* us to return. We preferred encouragement rather than permission, and this had to come from her heart. Literally, Mom would have to initiate the idea and then encourage our return. Even for parents who are healthy and have their spouse at their side, it is tough to have your children (and grandchildren) so far away.

11. We would need to return annually. We believed annual visits from us and the grandchildren would boost Mom emotionally. Chronic pain is emotionally draining, and annual visits would lift her spirits better than our traditional two or three year stretches between furloughs. The expense of transporting five people to and from Africa every year was enormous, and very few churches could or would foot that bill.

This was our list of eleven necessary impossibilities. We began praying for them regularly and watching for a reply.

Back at CDR, we were preparing for our first retreat season. Winterizing buildings and booking groups kept us occupied, but the stress was much less than that initial fall, and the pace was much more relaxed than the summer's tempo. Still, we were busy every day and active in our prayers for the camp's needs along with our 'list of eleven impossibilities.' We shared none of this with anyone, not even with family. About the time we started praying through the list of eleven, my brother shared some news: "I'm getting married!" Shocked (and in awe), we celebrated his announcement to marry a young woman he'd met at Camp Deer Run years earlier, Lisa Sutherland. On December 29th, 1990, I stood as his best man and our son Daniel was ring bearer at their wedding! In four months, impossibility #1 was marked off the list. We grew hopeful but continued to keep the existence of our list private.

Around that same time, I was invited to assist two US church leaders on a trip to Kenya as their translator. Since the event would be completed before summer registration began, I was available (and excited). I only needed to make one adjustment to my January schedule -- the design and publication of camp brochures. Because of the February departure date, I scheduled a late January meeting with Jay. Jay Spell had volunteered his printing services and skill to camp for several years and was willing to help a few weeks ahead of normal this time. On the day I arrived at his office, he was busy with another customer, so I waited in the lobby. A friendly elderly gentleman walked up to me and introduced himself as Jay's father, Earl. We struck up a conversation about Camp Deer Run, which led to an explanation of why I was in their office ahead of schedule this year. He was very curious about our former years in Kenya, and I had only told him a little about the work we'd done there and about our team when he totally shocked me.

"Steve, I am an elder at Shiloh Road Church. Our congregation has been working hard to pay off our facility for the last four years. Meanwhile, we've also been praying that God would lead us to a family we could support in an international mission. Would you come by and visit with us when you return from your trip?" I suppose I stammered some reply. I don't actually remember what I said, but I do clearly remember driving home wondering, "How did he get the idea that we might EVER return to Kenya? I never even came close to suggesting it!"

I told Donna, and of course, our hearts raced at the prospect that God might be answering another of those impossible prayers. Practically though, there was no time to think or talk about it much; there were loose ends to tie up and packing to do over the next couple of days before departure to Kenya. However, the conversation picked up energy upon my return home three weeks later.

"Hi Steve," the phone conversation began. "This is Earl Spell. How did your trip go?" Afraid that in some way I might have unintentionally influenced Mr. Spell in our first meeting, I'd decided not to contact him. Instead, I concluded that if God were in it, He would nudge Mr. Spell to call me… and now he had! I could hardly believe what was happening. I'd been back in the States less than three days! "Yes, it was a great trip. Thank you for asking," I replied, trying to sound calm and friendly without revealing the dizzying excitement inside me. "Good. Glad to hear it," he affirmed. "Well, Steve, we want to see if you can come see us here at Shiloh soon. We are interviewing several families and I'd like you to meet with us. When could you come?" Over the next weeks, we arranged the date, met with the eldership, and then promptly got busy with preparations for summer camp. Still, we never mentioned that we might be willing, able, or thinking about returning to Kenya. We met with them, only sharing information about missions in general and how we'd worked in Kenya before our time at Deer Run. It was an odd affair because they never actually asked if we'd be interested in returning to Africa, and we had never insinuated that we might be. The meeting was relaxed and felt more like an advisory meeting in which we were offering them advice on making their selection than it did an interview. They had lots of questions, and we shared from our past experience -- giving them ideas on what sort of mission work and missionaries they might want to consider in making a determination. Again, it was a very generic sort of conversation about missions, and not at all about us specifically or even Africa specifically. It was a tad surreal, to be honest. Yet, more was to come -- equally as inexplicable.

Billy Ray Dean is a Deer Run icon. Billy Ray had been one of my camp counselors when I was a boy, and he was on my board of directors. So seeing him stroll across the campground a few weeks later was not unusual. This particular morning, however, as I greeted him, he asked something that was totally unexpected: "Steve, tell me about your job."

Since I had no context for his question, I told him what was involved in managing and directing the corporation. It took about half an hour. He then said, "We need to give Doug a call." Doug Williams had been a camper at CDR beginning when he was nine years old. He'd served on the staff at every leadership level except the one I now held. He was, at the time of Billy Ray's visit, busy working in British Columbia in missions. For all those reasons, Billy Ray felt Doug would be a great replacement for me. The ironic thing is that I never implied that a replacement would be needed! How Billy Ray got the notion that we might want or be able (due to Mom's condition) to leave Deer Run remains a mystery to me to this day. All I know is that I answered his questions. Billy Ray contacted Doug, and Doug called me a couple of days later. "Steve, tell me about your job." Doug flew down and visited us at camp before summer camp began. Several weeks later, around mid-summer, the board of directors offered him the position of camp director. He accepted. I was out of a job; though ironically, no one had asked me if I was leaving. No one at camp appeared to be unhappy, at all, with our work. Yet, apparently, no one thought this was awkward (except me). Everyone had come to the assumption that we were leaving. It is now 25 years after that summer and I still have no physical or logical explanation. I can only credit the working of God for planting the notion in everyone's mind. Bizarre.

By this point, the camp was buzzing and I was blindingly busy 24/7. There wasn't time to stop and assess what was happening or think about what was next, until two weeks later when I received a phone call from none other than Earl Spell.

"Steve, this is Earl Spell."

"Hello, Brother Spell. Good to hear from you," I replied.

"Well Steve, I have good news. The elders have met and the congregation has decided on our mission program. Our church would like to sponsor your family to Africa."

Wow. Full support by one congregation! Another item off the list, and totally through prayer.

Within three days of his call, five other area congregations had heard about our sponsorship and contacted Shiloh asking to join the effort! These five fully financed our Work Fund (funds for airfare, operating expenses, etc. totaling $1500.00 per month). In three days, without a single fundraising letter, appeal for assistance, or mention of our hopes, we were fully funded. Obviously, God had worked in and through many of us, and it was exhilarating, but we tried to remain calm, knowing that there were still several more items on our prayer list -- all nigh unto impossible. Keep in mind that throughout this process, we had remained largely bystanders and observers. When asked to visit with the Shiloh Road elders, I had done so. Likewise, when asked about my job, I had answered. And when my job was offered to another person, without even a single conversation about my resignation, I did not balk. Now, in a little more than one month, he would be moving to Texas, but a huge question remained, "Where would Doug live?" CDR had land, but none suitable or accessible for housing. The board had no plan that I was aware of. I continued, however, to pray for land and resources for a house.

It was a very normal July morning. The camp mess hall was clanging with silverware, buzzing with chatter, and full of kids. I joined them for a quick bowl of cereal when a camper's mother walked over to my table and took a seat across from me. Her inquiry was another unexpected stunner.

"Steve, where is Doug going to live?"

"Sharon, I don't know."

"Well, I saw some land for sale just outside the gate at camp. Do you know who owns it?"

I did know. I'd been asking God for it for three years. Yet, my reply belied none of this. I simply said, "Yes, the Dean family."

"Find out what they want for it and let me know."

"Okay. I'll work on it today."

The entire tract for sale was about 90 acres, but she wondered if the family might sell only the 15-acre section immediately outside camp's gates. I told her I'd find out. She said, "Okay. Thank you."

That was it. She left to be with her son and I finished my cereal. There was no commitment, no expectation, just the inquiry, but enough to stir the imagination and raise hope.

With almost two full weeks of camp remaining, I was too busy to invest much time or energy into Sharon's inquiry. Billy Ray Dean helped me by talking with the owners of the property. They agreed to sell only the 15 acres to camp, and Billy Ray passed that information on to Sharon. A few days later Sharon called back with a proposal. "Okay. We can buy the land and give it to the camp. Now, I want to know, can you do this in some way that it is actually a prepayment of my kids' camp fees for the next several years?" I hadn't done this sort of thing before, so I needed to run it by someone who could advise me on the legalities of such an arrangement. I simply answered her, "I'll have to check and let you know."

It was a fair offer. It was a mom trying to gain the best for both the camp and her family. It sounded like a win-win for the camp and Sharon's family, but there was only one problem: a 501(c)3 organization cannot accept donations in exchange for goods or services. If she and her husband wanted or needed to claim this as a donation, they could not also receive credit for their kid's camp fees. I badly wanted this land deal to happen, and we were so close. I really tried to think of an ethical and legal scenario for it to be possible, but in the end, my conscience, and the law, prohibited her offer. She'd have to choose whether the tax write-off was more beneficial or the credit for the boys

-- which would never amount to the size of the donation she was considering anyway. I worried that it would be a deal breaker. In fact, I felt like it would, but honoring God is always the best way. When I explained the situation to her, she listened and then asked for some time to think about it. She didn't think long, but called back quickly with enthusiasm in her voice, "Okay, Steve. We'll buy the land!" Deer Run received a check for $15,000.00 on September 6th, 1992. Sharon's sacrificial response to God's nudge was perfect for that moment and for something 25 years in the future! In 2016 I spoke at a special event for Camp Deer Run in which it was announced that $1,400,000.00 would be invested in a new dining room and offices complex. That complex was to be built on the very parcel of land that Sharon purchased in 1992. Meanwhile, Doug had a place for a house! Now we only needed a house! As this transpired in Texas, Doug and family were packing up in British Colombia and taking a huge step of faith of their own. Doug called, clearly excited. "Jim Bob (that was my camp name as a college staff member)! You won't believe this! We just sold our house here in B.C. on the first day, to the first looker, at our full asking price! It was literally on the market a few minutes!" Over the next few days, Doug and the board of directors discussed a plan for him to purchase a double-wide modular home and have it located on the new plot of ground Sharon had purchased a few days earlier. Amazing! The new director now had a house!!! To my surprise, the day before Doug's house was to be delivered, Clark Spencer, a former Deer Runner, offloaded a bulldozer and proceeded to clear and level a site for the new house. The next day, when the house was delivered, it was leveled and anchored while I watched on the sidelines as the dozer and its operator removed trees and moved mountains of soil.

The situation at Deer Run had come far from those days when our tools were a wrench and a lawn mower and I was the only one working. In my final newsletter to camp supporters on October 1, 1993, I wrote,

"Our mission is accomplished. Deer Run is physically redone, emotionally things are positive and upbeat, spiritually we have never had more serious or more godly staff members in the history of the camp, numerically both income and enrollment are at 35-year highs. In closing, Donna and I want to express our sincerest thanks to all of you who, when prompted by God's leading, gave and prayed and gave more. We

hope for Deer Run, you, and us, that these years will stand as a powerful testimony of God's generous willingness to answer our prayers."

[CDR campers & staff]

KENYA (1992 - 1995)

The Deer Run chapter of our lives was now officially completed, but our future was still unsettled. Only two matters remained on our list of eleven impossibilities, but they could be deal-breakers.

My mother had worked as a bookkeeper since I was a child, and her retirement plan rested in social security, but that benefit was still years away since she was now only 58. Out of necessity, she was working through her pain, but four to five hours at the office meant agonizing in bed until the next morning. Seven more years of this would be impossible. If there was a way her needs could be met without her continuing to suffer, we wanted to find it. All I knew to do was to ask the LORD for a salary sufficient to meet my family's needs and to 'retire' Mom until social security or disability began to contribute. To our delight, when talking with the Shiloh Road Church elders, they agreed to a salary sufficient to cover both those needs.

But what about Mom's emotional needs? That question was answered one evening while visiting at her home. Mom quietly slipped over by me and began, "Steve, I have thought about this and prayed about this." My mother never did anything without thinking through it a LOT. So, I knew she'd put in days and weeks of considering the pros and cons and outcomes of all sorts of scenarios before she approached us that evening. Her words were not offered on an emotional whim. "I want you and Donna to know that I'll be okay and that I am excited about you returning to Kenya. You have my blessing." Those were not easy words. They were words spoken only after much consideration and a full weighing of their costs. Sending your children to the opposite side of the globe is heart-wrenching for any parent, but how much more frightening given her circumstances? This is just one example of the way my mother formed and contributed to my faith throughout my lifetime. Though frail in body, she was strong in faith.

Ten down and one to go! The one and only remaining 'impossibility' was an annual furlough, which was unheard in our fellowship at the time. The expense of transporting a family of five from Africa EVERY year was great. Churches just didn't do that sort of thing. It wasn't viewed as responsible stewardship. Only a generation or so before us, missionaries to Africa had shipped their possessions packed in wooden boxes resting in beds of their pick-up trucks. Those wooden boxes were actually their pre-built coffins! These bulwarks stayed 30, 40, 50 years and died 'in the field.' In light of them, our request seemed weak and selfish, but we were convinced it was essential because we believed it would bring Mom comfort, a break from loneliness, and an opportunity to be with her only (at the time) grandchildren. Meanwhile, I could report to churches while also tending to house or automobile needs she might have, and Donna could relieve her of meal preparation for a few weeks. Also, it would give my brother and his wife a break from these duties, which they'd certainly need and deserve.

Our expectation was this arrangement would allow us to stay longer on the mission field. It was a good plan and included an agreement with my brother that they would care for her for five years in the event her health deteriorated again. This ensured us a minimum of five years on the field. Still, however, the matter had to be introduced to the Shiloh Road leadership... and they had to agree to it. We decided to tackle it at our first official meeting with the church leadership.

Seated around a conference table, the seven of us were clearly enthusiastic about the mission. The church's minister, Mike Warner, and the eldership were eager to be engaged in our work. It was truly a wonderful atmosphere. Only the angst of the annual return question tainted it for me. As was customary, a prayer was offered to open the meeting. There was an opening statement from one of the elders expressing their enthusiasm for the work and delight in having us on board. I felt the same, but before I could open my mouth (literally), the elder sitting across from me asked, "So, Steve, how often will you be coming home to report to us?" I could not believe it! THEY had broached the subject. I swallowed hard and prayed silently, "Lord, here it comes. Help me out."

Up to that moment, eleven of those impossible prayers had been offered, and ten had become reality -- without a word from us. What would it mean if the eleventh one did NOT come to fruition? Would it void the others? Should we continue if this door closed? All these questions raced through my mind simultaneously. I paused, then answered, "Well, we thought it would be good if we could return each year for a few weeks." Immediately, a voice from the eldership said, "Good! We were hoping to hear from you every year. It would be a great idea to have you all back here to report in person!" I sat amazed.

The Shiloh Road Church truly loved us and the mission to Kenya. I've never before or since seen or experienced the same euphoric level of enthusiasm and delight from a congregation. At this point, all eleven prayers had been answered, but as is always true with the God of grace, He did not stop here. Though it is nearly impossible to imagine, God went beyond our expectations -- far beyond.

A good brother and deacon at Shiloh Road, David Litton, accepted the role of liaison between the congregation and ourselves. In banking by trade, he had no qualms discussing finances. Standing in the foyer between the time of preaching and the time for Bible classes, David asked me, "So, how much money will you need to get started over there?" I actually hadn't thought about it. We'd been immersed in camp duties literally right up until two nights before. So, I did some quick calculations on the spot. I gulped and sheepishly said, "I imagine about $30,000 - $35,000." Now, after working with Deer Run's slim budget, that was a ton of money. However, vehicles in Kenya, even older used ones, could easily cost that entire amount. We would also need airfare and initial startup costs for permits, visas, temporary housing, etc. So, though a lot of money, my figures were pretty conservative. David shot back, without a blink, "Is that all? You'll need more than that," he encouraged. "It'll probably take more like $50,000. What do you think?" He hadn't batted an eye at that sum. I was speechless. Four years earlier, I had personally repaired the septic system at Deer Run due to a lack of $50 to hire someone to do it. Now, sums that I could hardly imagine were questioned as insufficient! Honestly, I liked this newer side of the journey.

Over the next few months we were busy meeting members (there were 700 of them), teaching classes on missions, and educating the entire congregation about the mission through different events and opportunities. One of my favorites (and the congregation's favorites) was "A Taste of Culture Banquet," where we introduced the idea of culture via a food fair. Booths with authentic international fare were decorated and manned by members who had experience with or were originally from some other culture. The members of the congregation visited the different booths, sampling foods from those places, looking at pictures from those locations, and asking questions and gathering information from the people at the booth. It was great fun and expanded the church's worldview.

As our departure neared, David masterminded a plan for raising the $50,000 in a SINGLE Sunday collection. David was excited; Donna and I were busy with the mission plans; the members were happy. All seemed blessed. Then came the day of the collection. It was electric. An air of excitement filled that Sunday service. I spoke. The elders and ministers supported and cheered on the Body. The 'regular' tithe was collected, and then the special Kenya Mission collection was taken. There was a closing prayer and the service dismissed. All who wanted to stay were invited to a church-wide fellowship meal as the funds were being tallied. The whole place buzzed as we laughed, ate, and waited to hear. Within a half-hour, David, the elders and ministers of the congregation, and those with them who had been counting the gifts entered the dining area. David was grinning. They called the room to order and prepared to make the announcement. "Well, you folks have done it again.

We expected you'd do everything that would be necessary to get the Meeks to Africa, but we, or at least some of us, didn't expect what this congregation has come to be guilty of a few times before -- you exceeded what was asked of you." Then, David brought in a huge 3' x 5' cardboard check. On it in the memo was written "The Meeks to Africa." The amount collected, above the regular donation, on a single Sunday was $75,000.00! When the final amount was announced, it was as if the home team had just scored the winning touchdown! The crowd cheered, high-fived, laughed, whooped, and cheered. Shiloh Road was unlike any church we had ever known. For sure, we knew they were directly from the LORD's good hand.

[Meeks family - 1992]   [Meeks collection sunday at Shiloh Road]

A few weeks later, an entire houseful of new furnishings and appliances already in a shipping container on its way to Kenya, and our farewells said, David and a small Shiloh Road delegation escorted us to DFW airport, where we shared tears, a final goodbye, and a last prayer. 30-plus hours later, we were enjoying four o'clock tea and biscuits (cookies) at the quaint and familiar Mennonite Guest House in Nairobi with our dear friends and former teammates, Larry and Holly Conway. Above us, the sun was warm and healing. We sat in a garden-portrait of color. A manicured lawn and a clear blue sky provided the canvas for a breathtakingly perfect scene where red bougainvillea and mature purple jacaranda mixed color with fragrance, and a flame tree bled bright red. Pied crows accented the tropical cacophony of a feathered orchestra performing around us. In this blissful context, our children played and giggled for the joy of a tire swing shared in the reunion with childhood buddies. My feelings were inexpressible. It must have been much like the feeling a fish, flopping on a sandy bank, gasping for breath, has the instant it re-enters the water -- I'm-back-where-I'm-supposed-to-be! Neither Donna nor I recall another day quite like it; something of heaven was in it.

The next two years were challenging, as is almost all foreign living and ministry, but overall we were blessed beyond our greatest imaginations. During those years Daniel broke both collarbones, there was one miscarriage, and Donna lost her grandmother, but overall our lives were terrific! Shiloh Road continued to amaze us with their generosity and deep concern for the mission's ministry and us. I sent a short video report to the Shiloh Road Church a few months after our arrival, which they aired to the entire congregation one Sunday morning. Afterward, one of the members phoned me, "Hey Steve!" I answered, "Hi! Wow. Good to hear from you!" (International phone calling was a much more rare event at that time than it is currently.) We chatted a bit and then he got to the point. "Steve, we loved the video. But I noticed just how rough those roads are, and was wondering if, and don't think I'm crazy, but I was wondering if maybe one of those ultra-light planes might make it easier for you to reach those villages." Most missionaries struggle to acquire a vehicle; we were being offered a plane! I couldn't help but be amazed anew at the exceptional generosity and concern of this congregation. We had the best missionary-care situation I've ever heard of, which made it even more difficult, two and a-half years later, to return to the States and end it.

Our return to Kenya was glorious. I truly loved going out to the villages, teaching, helping, advising, and fellowshipping with the saved and the lost alike. The Kalenjin people, whom we served, are such a hospitable people. They took us in as friends when we were strangers and as family once we had become friends. Those were sweet times for our family, our team, and our children. The missionary families in Kenya at that time were many -- almost 40. We met once a month for a potluck and to fellowship, catch up on news, and coordinate to help one another in ministry. Looking back, those were the glory days of our life... if only they had not been cut short.

Kenya (1992 - 1995)

[Kenya Team]

[Kenya Oriok]

[Elders visit to Kenya]

Between April and September of 1995 dark clouds gathered over our joyful season in Kenya. The plan had been for Mom to stay with my brother for the first five years if her condition deteriorated. After that, we would return to the US and take over her care. In April Mom revealed that her condition was getting more difficult. Of course, this was unsettling news. We had done all we knew possible to create a living situation conducive to her wellbeing. The Shiloh Road men had even invested time and money helping remodel a house she had purchased near her brother and sister-in-law. This too was our collective effort to provide a comfortable and supportive environment for her. Meanwhile, my brother and I discussed Mom's rapidly changing condition, and the possible need for our "five-year minimum" understanding to be put into play sooner than anticipated. Neither of us expected this so suddenly. As newlyweds, they were hardly prepared for such a daunting responsibility. All these variables considered, our backup plan was no longer a viable option.

However, in our optimism, Donna and I followed through on an arrangement we had already made with our coworkers, Stephen and Claudia Greek. They were relocating to the Unites States, and we, intending to live in Eldoret for years to come, made arrangements to move into their larger house. Since the rainy season was approaching, I even hired men to help prepare a garden site. However, by mid-May, it was clear that our contingency plan was not going to work, that Mom needed us again, and that we would need to leave before harvest. The conversation that decided everything came when the phone rang.

"Hello," I answered.

"Steve?" It was my mother's voice. She sounded on the verge of tears.

"Yes, Mom. It's me. I can hear you. Is everything all right?"

Always one to deflect attention from herself, Mom avoided a direct answer by inquiring, "Are you all okay?"

"Yes. We are all fine," I pressed. "What's up?"

"Well, son," she began slowly, "I'm not doing too well, and… I don't think I can manage here anymore without help. I really need you to come home." She began to cry. Her heart was breaking because she knew that what she was asking would require us to forsake the ministry to which we were devoted and leave a life we dearly loved. But Donna and I knew in our hearts what we must do. We told her we would be there as soon as we possibly could. Mom had bravely coped with chronic pain for years, but now it was crippling. It was time for direct help. All along, we had kept our missions co-coordinator with Shiloh Road, Gregg Grubb, informed of our thinking and Mom's condition. Now that the decision was obvious, it was with Greg that we first shared our plans to return to the US. Supporters in the US were quickly informed, and arrangements for our return began. As uncertain as our future was, one thing was perfectly clear -- the pages ahead of us would not read as we had imagined only a few weeks before.

Some may imagine that a return to the comforts of America, the fellowship of loved ones, and the ease of living in one's home culture would be welcome. It was not so for us. Our hearts were in Africa. It was our second home and its people our friends, church, and family. Jesus promised that He would give his disciples hundreds of Mothers and Fathers and homes, and He had fulfilled it for us. We were returning home, yes, but we were leaving family. Saying goodbye to our team, friends, work, and life in Kenya was like tearing away a limb; we would limp without it. Moving is a challenge even under normal conditions, but under ours at that time, it was monumental. Donna was too far advanced in her pregnancy to travel. This left the lion's share of the relocation responsibilities on me. By itself, this was overwhelming, but my broken heart compounded it all. With joy (and no complications) Benjamin Tyler Meeks was born to us in Eldoret, Kenya, on June 11, 1995. His middle name was given in honor of our sweet sponsoring church in Tyler, Texas. We rejoiced, but we couldn't savor the moment as much as we would have wanted, because a LOT had to happen quickly.

For the next three months, we scrambled. First, over the next six weeks, we sold all our furniture, equipment, vehicles, and appliances, bought tickets, and packed our bags. We sold all that we owned personally as well as the appliances and furnishings that Shiloh had purchased for us. Once back in the States, funds from all the items purchased by Shiloh were returned to the church's general mission fund. As for personal possessions, there were a few items of sentimental value that we crated and shipped back to the States, otherwise, we returned with our suitcases and the cash from the sale of our things. In the midst of this, Donna recovered from having a baby, hosted groups at our house who came to wish us farewell, and attended many of the good-bye ceremonies at each of the village churches. Tears were shed among our teammates and coworkers. Then, in late August, we were aboard a KLM airliner en route to the States. As exhilarating as our entry to Kenya had been, our return to the US was correspondingly depressing. With children in tow and the task of reporting ahead, there was no time to grieve. September and October were a blur. Though outwardly we smiled at every church service and remained cordial through every conversation, inwardly we mourned the death of the life we'd so very much loved. Yes, our bodies were in America, but in truth, our hearts remained in Africa.

[Ellen & Donna saying farewell]

Shiloh graciously assisted us with our relocation by offering used furnishings and a continuation of our salary for several months. As wonderful as everyone was, I didn't have a job, a home, or a vision. Yes, it was stressful. No, I didn't like it. But we needed to be nearer my mother to care for her. Not much was clear beyond that except that God was good and I knew He was near. It was a crucible time, but only the beginning.

[Meeks family back from Kenya]

THE WILL OF GOD

Discerning the will of God is difficult, but I've come to believe the difficulty is largely due to two fundamental misunderstandings. First, we imagine the will of God is a mystery, when in fact His general will is clear -- that all men should be rescued (saved) from the grip of rebellion (sin) and separation (death). God's will is not a secret that we must discover. Scripture makes known His general will to every man.

Second, we believe that God has a specific will (assignment) for each individual (or at least for us) beyond His general will. This is difficult to support from Scripture. A specific will or task for every individual is rare in Scripture. When one does exist it is demonstrably clear. For example, Ananias was chosen to approach Saul of Tarsus. Ananias knew this to be the specific will of God since he was given the name of the street, the homeowner, and the man he was to meet. In fact, the exact words he was to speak to Saul were dictated to him (Acts 9:10ff).

In other examples, Paul was told specifically that he would be a messenger to the Gentiles. It wasn't necessary for Paul to guess whether God wanted him to teach Gentiles (Acts 9:15). Mary was told by the angels that she would have a Son and what to name Him (Luke 1:30-31). The demon-possessed man who lived among the Geresenes was told not to leave his home area but to stay in his hometown (Mark 5:19).

The list goes on. For example, the woman caught in adultery was told, "Go and sin no more" (general will of God), but Elizabeth and Zechariah were told they would have a son and that his name should be John (specific will of God). Discerning the general will of God is not left to guesswork. Likewise, the specific will of God, when He has one for a person, is evident.

God's general will is revealed in the Bible -- though, on many levels, it is done in an almost playful clever way, like hunting eggs at Easter. It is clearly discoverable, but must be sought out. Scripture explains this by saying, "It is the glory of God to conceal a matter; to search out a matter is the glory of kings" (Proverbs 25:2). Jesus encourages us to "ask, seek, and knock." These three verbs are in the action tense, and they say something more like "keep on asking, keep on seeking, and be knocking all the time." God wants us to know His will, but He wants us to invest ourselves by hunting for it.

Now when God selects an individual for a specific task, He doesn't expect that person to guess at His grand scheme with only the most subjective hints. He sends an angel or speaks to him directly in a vision or a dream. Again, God reveals His general will clearly in Scripture to each of us; however, on the rare occasion when He has a specific task for an individual, He communicates through angels, visions, dreams, or a visitation.

Both His general will and His specific will are delivered supernaturally, and both are clear. "For since the message spoken through angels was binding, and every violation and disobedience received its just punishment" (Hebrews 2:2). In fact, they are very clear. For example, Paul, the one specifically tasked with taking the Gospel to the Gentiles, tried to enter Phrygia but was kept out by the Holy Spirit. Then Jesus prevented them from entering Bithynia. Paul later had a vision of a man in Macedonia and concluded that God had called them to preach the gospel to them (Acts 16:6-10).

Having pondered this topic for many decades, my understanding is that, if and when God has a specific wish or job for me, He will let me know through a vision, a visitation, or an angel. If He does not, then I must conclude that He has no specific will for me at that time, and I am free to carry out His general will as I see best. However, I must be clear that this was not my understanding at the time we returned to the US. At that time, we were trying to piece together the fragments of 'evidence' before us and to discern whether it was His will for us to live in Tennessee or elsewhere. The rest of this story is what happened when we pursued obedience to what we 'discerned' to be His specific will for us. In retrospect, what I take away from those years is much less about His specific will or our ability to discern it, and much more about His mercy and grace in dealing with His followers, whether they understand these concepts or not.

With that as our backdrop, we entered the States with an uncertain future. Only three months before, our vision for the future involved life and ministry in Africa. We had never considered a stateside alternative, and during our whirlwind transition, little energy or time had been available to consider or explore our options. There had simply been too much to do in leaving Kenya to think about America… until we landed.

Within a few days after our arrival, three ministry opportunities surfaced. In West Texas, a member of the college of missions at a Christian university spoke with me about integrating missions into other colleges within the university. On one hand, influencing university-age men and women was attractive, but on the other hand, the transition from the Kenyan Acacia's shade to the Texas college's classroom was as great as the miles between them. It was simply too much too soon. We weren't emotionally ready to make such a great cultural leap. Our experiences, skills, and temperament were better suited for something less academic and more hands-on. We decided against this option. There was some discussion of planting a church in Northeast Texas among the growing population of immigrant workers and their families. It was one we liked, and it matched our training and experience, but extenuating circumstances portended roadblocks in that direction, so we decided against it also. A small group of families in New Jersey offered a third option. They asked that we launch a house church near Camden. We drove there to see for ourselves. Immediately, two things were apparent: Camden was not Kenya, and we were not urban missionaries. I remember being physically dizzied by the blur of activity and noise. We loved the house-church idea, but this wasn't a fit either.

Of course, at this point, time was running out and pressure to make a decision was mounting. The trip to New Jersey occurred in the final week of the reporting period we'd set for ourselves. It was time to move ahead, but we were undecided on where 'ahead' would be. Hours of discussion followed as Donna and I drove from New Jersey to Texas. Then, about 6 hours into our drive, a new possibility came to mind. We made an impromptu phone call to friends Bruce and Dale Woodall, who lived near the border of Kentucky and Tennessee. It was not far off our planned travel route to Texas. The call went through and we left a voice message asking if they might be open for a surprise visit. Shortly, Dale returned our call with an enthusiastic, "Yes! Please, come!" We adjusted our course to include their small town -- Jellico, Tennessee. Entering Jellico, a prayer, known only to Donna and myself, was offered, *"Lord, if this is the place, give our friends the thought to invite us to come here."* During our visit with them, we were very careful about giving absolutely no hint that we were talking to God about them or the region. If anything happened it would clearly be motivated by Forces beyond us.

During the first two days, our hosts introduced us to various friends and colleagues -- sharing with us their life and experiences in the mountains of Tennessee. We told the story of our years in Kenya as well as recent events and the three opportunities we'd explored. Never -- not one time -- was the notion of involvement in Appalachia suggested until the last evening when, after the meal, Dale abruptly offered an invitation that would change the course of our lives for the next two decades. She asked, "We are so busy at the clinic addressing physical needs that we don't have time or energy to minister after hours to people's spiritual needs. Why don't you come here?"

The next day, driving to Texas, other than the need for diaper changes or meal concerns, we talked about only one thing -- their invitation to Appalachia. We stopped at a rest area immediately across the Texas state line. After 13 hours in a cramped car, the kids needed to spend some energy and we all needed to breathe fresh air. I needed to pray.

I reminded Donna, "You know we asked God to have them invite us if He wanted us there."

She replied, "And that's what happened!"

"I guess we're moving to Tennessee?"

"Yes," she said, "I think we should."

It may appear we made our decision by "throwing out a fleece." It was not the case. We made our decision by following and applying guidelines from the book *Experiencing God* by Henry Blackaby, which involved three elements: consideration of the experiences, gifts, and talents God has already given; the godly counsel of others; and personal peace. Our experience and skills over the years had been with church planting in rural communities, with the poor, and across cultures. Those who knew us best, and whom we respected most, had unanimously encouraged us to stick with church planting. Even though the other three opportunities were worthy, the Appalachian prospect was the only one which brought us peace. Blackaby's guidelines were at the core of our final decision. Dale's invitation simply reinforced what we had already suspected was the direction we should go. One other matter contributed to tipping the scales toward Appalachia. Not inconsequentially, the month before my mother had called us in Africa, Donna and I watched the video series "Christie," which is about a Christian teacher who lived in Appalachia. I distinctly recall offhandedly remarking -- but never imagined it happening -- "*15 or 20 years down the road we might retire and work there.*" Our hearts were already being softened for Appalachia. At the state line in Texarkana, our new direction was decided. Our friends in Tennessee needed a church planter's help, we needed to get to work, and the opportunity met all the criteria in Blackaby's book. Both Donna and I immediately experienced a peace and excitement that had been missing since the day Mom called us in Kenya. Dale's invitation cannot be dismissed as 'coincidental.' Her action was a very specific answer to our secret prayer. It became the first small pebble among many in our bag of prayer answers that would span the next two decades.

While religion was prevalent and churches plentiful in the mountains, the holy life that Christ produces was far too rare. We arrived there believing that God desired to reach two groups: those who had a form of religion but did not have a dynamic relationship with God; and those who, for whatever reasons, rejected the existing communities of faith, but who would likely follow Jesus if they saw an authentically lived version of Him. Our dream was greater than a single church plant; we envisioned a 'movement' and asked God to produce hundreds of communities of faith in rural towns and townships running the entire length of the Appalachian Mountain range, eastward down the mountains, and across the ocean into Europe. Would He answer? Only time would tell. In the meantime, the more practical question was, "How would we survive?" The invitation to Appalachia had not included a salary. So what about our income? It was a matter we weighed heavily before deciding on Jellico. We took encouragement from knowing the character of God. Would the God who commanded that farmers feed their oxen and that employers pay workers their daily wages fail to care for His own laborers' needs? We knew that He not only would not fail to provide, but He *could not* fail. Faith is always a matter of moving into that which we believe to be true before we experience it as fact. So, by faith, six and a half months after Mom's phone call to us in Kenya, on December 10, 1995, we waved a final goodbye to our friends and family in Texas who had been our financial and moral supporters. There was no salary, no assurance of success, and only our personal discernment based on Blackaby's guidelines that God ordained it. Donna expressed it best, *"We were leaving security, but feeling peace."* Three days later I turned off the engine and parked our Ryder Truck at 203 W. Florence Ave. in Jellico, Tennessee, breathed a sigh of relief and offered a prayer to Him who would now be our Provider. For mid-December, it was an unseasonably warm and sunny day, but not to last -- storms were on the way. The next pages would not be what we imagined.

[Our Ryder truck and cars]

JELLICO (1995 - 2017)

The house on Florence Avenue was just large enough for the seven of us to squeeze into, but it was an adequate starting place, and we were very thankful to finally be out of suitcases! Dale, who'd invited us to Appalachia only a few weeks earlier, had made all the arrangements for us: getting the utilities connected, and cleaning the house. A Christmas wreath on our front door welcomed us, and inside, a tree twinkled with lights. In the kitchen, a decorative holiday cloth invitingly covered a dining table. The kids shrieked with delight. Donna and I were humbled and blessed. That wonderful old house on Florence Avenue would be our home for the next five years, but with neighbors like this, the time would pass all too quickly. More stones clinked as they fell into our bag.

The house itself was elderly -- sagging a bit in the middle. Modifications had been made ad hoc over its years. An uninsulated area over the porch opened to the boys' bedroom and was useful in summer as a bedroom for Hannah. The low ceiling gave her the feel of being in a girl-size dollhouse. On extremely cold winter nights we moved her into the boys' or our room. Otherwise, the porch loft was perfect for a four-year-old who loved playing house. Upstairs, the low ceilings and close quarters were more kid-size than adult, which was a dream-come-true hideout for our boys. On the other hand, the ceiling was a bit low for my 6'2". Only in the center of the room, beneath the roof peak, was I able to stand without bending. The ceiling met a 2' knee wall on either side, so our bed's frame could not fit flush against the wall. So for five years, our mattress lay directly on the floor. Downstairs, a kitchen, washroom, small sitting room, dining room, and bedroom (for Mom) squeezed into about 800 square feet. A single bathroom had been added to the house off the dining room. Originally the house had lacked indoor plumbing, but an indoor bathroom had been added about eight to ten steps from Mom's room, which was a terrific convenience and an especially considerate kindness from the LORD. A large wild apple tree grew in the backyard. The kids loved its tart fruit. The front yard had just enough room to park our two cars. This, then, is where we began. It was God's first provision for us, and we thanked Him. Many pages of good memories would be written from that precious spot, and many pebbles added to our bag of answered prayer.

After moving my family and mother into the Florence Street house, my next order of business was finding work, which I naively assumed would not be a problem. Though not skilled in a marketable trade or profession, I had marketable qualities: honest, articulate, educated, healthy, hardworking, and a quick learner. I figured, *"Within six months I'll be employed and up and running with the church planting."* Soon, though, a title for the next chapter of our life became clear: "Overly Optimistic."

Since the 1960s, rural Appalachia has been a low-income, high-unemployment region within the Unites States, lagging behind national income averages even in booming economic years. Jellico, I soon concluded, must be America's epicenter for economic depression. There just weren't any jobs.

As a missionary, I had no training or experience for secular industry but was somewhat experienced as a self-starter. With no jobs available, I attempted various types of self-employment -- often working at several simultaneously. I tried multi-level marketing, sign painting, book writing, carpentry, investing, and agriculture. Meanwhile, I also applied at Rite Aid, the State Park, and Taylor's Machine Shop. I interviewed at a Wal-Mart distribution center 65 miles away. I tried everything that had even a remote chance of providing income for us. There were many 16-18 hour days traveling as far as Texas and

Arkansas to promote discounted phone service (my multi-level job) which yielded no profit and often a financial loss. Though we lived very frugally, only three times during those first three years did my monthly earnings meet our expenses for that month. As a result, our savings dwindled; correspondingly, my stress grew, and I questioned the sanity (or insanity) of moving to Appalachia. It seemed like we'd boarded a sinking ship.

Again, I'm racing ahead in the story. The accounts of God's provisions are detailed in the pages ahead, but for now, understand that the character and promises of God, as revealed in Scripture, were what sustained us throughout our Appalachian journey. If comfort, ease, and quick answers had been our foundation, we'd have left that first year. The anchor to which our boat was tethered in these storms was the faith that God, who expected His people to feed their work animals, would certainly provide for those who invested their energies and time doing His work.

We had some history with God. Our previous experiences anchored us. He had provided for our needs at Camp Deer Run. He had provided for our needs in Kenya by surprising us with gifts of goods and unsolicited financial gifts from others. Throughout our first three years in Jellico, God provided for the bulk of our financial needs in similar ways. It begs the question, "Was this coincidence or Providence?"

1995 - The Florence Avenue House

December 15

God provided a three-bedroom rental house for $300 per month. The timing was, of course, perfect. Dale Woodall worked hard preparing all the water, electric, and telephone arrangements prior to our arrival.

These provisions are God's first. Now, I will begin searching for work.

Jellico is small now, but a few decades ago it was a coal mining boomtown. I learned that the name 'Jellico' is a regional corruption of 'Angelica,' an herb that grows in abundance in the surrounding mountains. The name was first applied to the mountains to the west and to the mountains' main drainage, Jellico Creek, which empties into the Cumberland River near Williamsburg, Kentucky. In the early 1880s, a high-quality bituminous coal was discovered in the Jellico Mountains, and with the completion of railroad tracks to the area in 1883, coal mines quickly sprang up throughout the area. The city of Jellico was initially founded as Smithburg in 1878 but changed its name to 'Jellico' in 1883 to capitalize on the growing popularity of Jellico coal. The city was incorporated on March 7, 1883.

Throughout the 1890s and early 1900s, Jellico was one of the most productive coal fields in Kentucky and Tennessee. In 1906, a parked railroad car packed with dynamite exploded in the town center, killing eight and destroying or damaging the commercial buildings along Main Street. The town quickly recovered, however, and many of the buildings standing today within the downtown area date from this recovery period. I learned from Wikipedia that at its peak, Jellico boasted upwards of 10,000 residents, an opera house, a members-only golf club, and Tennessee's first private airport.

Today, Jellico shares much in common with a lengthy list of townships from Georgia to Pennsylvania that have fallen from their former glory; however, we sense that God has selected Jellico as a strategic point for reasons yet to unfold.

December 19
My first interview was today in Barbourville, KY. There is rumor that a factory is opening in Jellico soon. After the interview, the manager offered me a position as a supervisor! This was more than I'd expected, but so were the job requirements. The position required being on call 24/7. The shift he offered me was from 3 p.m. to 12 midnight. These hours would prohibit me from prime family time during the week and perhaps weekends. The company clearly needed someone they could train and depend upon for the long term, and I knew that such a schedule would only be temporary for me -- if possible at all. Believing that ministry will one day consume all my time, I was transparent and told him I could not be counted on to be available over the long term and added that I also had to

decline since I had children and could not be the father they would need if I were not available to them more than this position would allow.

So, I declined the offer as supervisor but left my application for any lesser position that offered daytime hours. Having stood firm on principles of family-first and full disclosure, I passed on the possibility of securing one of the highest paying jobs available in or near Jellico today. I am not afraid; God is also firm on His principles.

December 29
Following the interview in Barbourville, God began a shower of blessings. These gifts were sent to us in December, though we solicited none of them.

- M. and S.B. $100
- Holly Lake Church $1000
- J. and D.M. $150
- M. and M.A. $50
- K.I.M. $200
- E. and F.W. $50
- D. and J.M.—a ham
- T. and D.H. $205
- B. and D.W. $28
- Shiloh Road Church gave a resettlement gift of $6300.
- Leaving Texas, many individuals offered us used furniture and other items we needed for furnishing our Tennessee home.

By this time, we could see Mom's health was worse than we had realized. She described her chronic pain as "burning from the inside out." Doctors had not determined a cure or even come to a consensus as to its cause. She consumed a regimen of medications daily in an effort to modify her pain, enable her to sleep, and help her cope with the accompanying depression. These delivered limited benefits, but also some major negative side effects. For example, her muscles twitched so violently in her sleep that to prevent her from falling off her bed, we kept one side of it against a wall while I slept in a chair on the other side. Sometimes she would wake in a state of confusion. Being close by allowed me to reassure her, lend help with a walk to the bathroom, or get her a drink. Admittedly, it was a difficult season, but as difficult as it was for us, it was obviously more so for her.

December 30
This Christmas we were given two large boxes filled with new winter shoes, boots, and underclothing. A church in North Carolina heard of us and was moved by God to send these items!

Yesterday, we got news from Richard and Carolyn East in Texas. They'd been moved by the LORD to send us some support. Wanting to be completely forthcoming with them, I explained that there were some doctrinal differences between them and us. I explained, but in the end, they had no problem with those differences and assured us they'd continue sending gifts.

God is daily confirming to me that He is near and aware and involved. Also, for the past two mornings, I've felt compelled to lay prostrate before the Lord during my prayers as I pray for Mom. Yesterday she said, "Steve, today I've had one of those rare days when I've felt really good."

December 31
After they left our house today, we discovered Dan and Shar Swinehart had left a total of $160.00 cash on our pillows and refrigerator. Their note said that they intend to give regularly.

1996 - UNEMPLOYED

January 2
Bruce and Dale Woodall handed me a $600 check today. They said that after summarizing their year's income, this was excess.

A small payment of $13.25 arrived in the mail today. It was from the sale of some of our items we'd left in Kenya.

John Morrow sent the name of a prayer partner.

January 3
Received a gift of pastries! There were enough for four breakfasts from JR. His daughter dropped them off as she drove through on her way back to college.

Received a letter from our new friend in Texas, George K., saying he'd made a contribution to his church for us that would be sent soon.

January 4
The Sizemore family gave us a table and four chairs for the dining room. They're antique and very nice.

January 5
George K.'s gift arrived in the mail today. It was for $1000!

January 10
John Morrow sent $100 plus a list of 16 names of people who want our newsletter and will be praying for us!

January 12
Took Mom to Dr. Agnoli -- no change.

January 14
R. and G.S. sent $50 and a card with encouragement. M.E. sent $10. L. Adams -- whom we don't remember having met -- sent $50 and has chosen us as her 'project for the year.' She plans to send aid monthly.

January 25
I found a penny on the road while walking.

February 12
John Morrow sent $300. West and Lori S. sent $250.

March 12
In today's mail were a money order and a note. The note read, "Steve, God prompted us to give this." The postmark was from Colorado Springs, Colorado. The money order was for $500. We don't know anybody in Colorado Springs; I can't think of anyone we know in the state of Colorado!

April 30
Regina Social Club at Harding University sent a gift of $500. Nicole, the daughter of Fielden and Janet Allison, is in that club and suggested that they assist us. I knew her when she was an infant but have not been in contact since. Only God could have imagined such a thing as this.

May 6

I've been pushing very hard since June of '94 when we started preparations for reentry to the US. Beginning in January, my health began to suffer. Likely, it is stress related. I have struggled to establish an income through selling discounted telephone service, but I have not realized a single cent of profit. I've been telling myself that building a business takes time, but I need to see some benefits soon. Meanwhile, I will continue to 'work my fields' and look to the Lord of Harvests for a crop. Today, I spoke to the Lord for a long while about all of this.

It was amazing to watch God provide through so many people and with such surprise and variety. For example, we had not known George K. previously, but he and his wife, Barbara, would support us monthly for 15 years!

May 12
- George K. $100
- K. and S.H. $30
- A.C. $25
- Terry and Gina B. $15
- John M. $50
- Laura A. $50
- K.I.M. $200
- C.S. $60

May 16

At times we have experienced pleasures and privileges enjoyed by the world's wealthiest. As an example, for several months the Woodalls have paid for us to have a maid clean our house once a month. What a blessing from the Lord and a help to Donna! On those days, we live like royalty.

May 19

Ernie and Trudy Williams sent a gift of $500. They included

a note explaining that this was a special amount, but they intended to send $50 on a monthly basis. God has been sending gifts of $500 almost monthly from various unexpected sources.

May 23
I prayed for help today and had the thought that I should pray for 'singers.' I'm supposing that they will play a significant role in the progress of the Lord's Body in Appalachia. It seems that Appalachians have historically been gifted in this way. Music is possibly the heart language of these people. (*God answered this prayer on 11/08/00*)

June 10
Gift from R.G. of $25. We do not know R.G. or how he knows us.

July 7
David and Joan McRay gave us an air-conditioner and two ceiling fans! It's been uncomfortably hot, so these were special gifts for specific needs.

July 10
Received an invitation to speak at a youth event. They paid me $500 for speaking and reimbursement for travel. I did not ask for any remuneration.

August 11
What a surprise! Russ Dudrey sent $200. I'd neither seen nor heard from Russ in 16 years!

September 16
I've been delinquent in recording our gifts. We have received decreasing amounts each month. The past two months have hardly reached $900 per month. It has pressed

me to become more sober about my dependence upon God. I've been sent to my knees again in earnest. The result has been a greater and purer dependence upon God to provide our needs. I've tried -- I mean I have *really* tried to produce an income through marketing phone service and also sign painting, but the result has been a $0 net profit. Literally, only through God's provisions have we made it this far. God is my strength.

September 17
Finally a profit! Blessed today with a $37 check from phone sales. I also realized $2455.00 earnings today through an investment in a mutual fund I made several months ago.

The discounted phone service business was not supporting us, but I still held a conviction that we should be in Appalachia as vocational missionaries and by it provide an example of godly manhood. With the government providing medicine, food, shelter, and education, a percentage of local men felt little urgency to work. Welfare had destroyed initiative and destroyed any sense of personal responsibility in so many young men who were capable of working. Between the government and a string of local charities many (NOT ALL) men were robbed of motivation to join the work force. I could see why the easy way was chosen. What I'd been doing to this point was far more difficult and actually, less profitable. In some ways, I couldn't blame them.

As much as I wanted it to be otherwise, the struggle to continue searching for work was growing more emotionally difficult. After months of effort with little to show for it, I fell into a diminishing sense of that I-am-able-to-conquer self-esteem I'd brought with me. A dissenting voice told me, "Today won't be any different. Give up." Each day, the effort to look for employment seemed a steeper climb. Despair knocked, but I pushed past my feelings and continued searching for or creating work. It was during one of these financially difficult seasons when my brother, Danny, visited.

On his second day with us, Danny drove the five blocks into Jellico for a soda.

About three hours later, he returned… with a smile on his face.

"Come on, let's go!" he said.

"Go where?" I asked.

"I don't know where it is, but I've got a job in some place called 'Oneida.' Do you know where it is?"

I could not believe it! After over a year of hustling in every way I could imagine I had found nothing of any significance, and now my brother, on only his second day in town, had landed a job!

The entire story unfolded as we drove to Oneida. He explained how on his way to get the soda he'd noticed a small car dealership in town and stopped in to ask if they needed their store windows painted. He had made lots of extra money in Texas painting those signs on storefronts and car windshields that read things like 'Low Miles!' and '$500 Rebate!' This time he'd done a double-dip and sold the local owner on the idea of putting some signage on the large glass windows across the front of his building as well as on his car windshields. In fact, the owner hired him to put a sign on the local store and another sign on his dealership in Oneida, Tennessee. Danny, my brother, was paid $500 for about four hours work.

The next day, I was a sign painter! On our return from Oneida I'd mined Danny's brain for a few tips, and after a day's practice on my Suburban's glass windows, I was on the streets of Jellico (there are only two) carrying $100 of paints and brushes. After offering a prayer, I literally went door to door down the business section of Jellico. It took about an hour to visit every shop and introduce myself and my service. The response was consistently, 'No,' until the next to the last shop; they wanted a sign!

September 23
It took 9 hours. The sun was behind me and really gave me a good burn on the back of my neck, but I found and completed

my first sign job. I prayed with almost every stroke that I wouldn't ruin this guy's window. When I was finished, my shirt soaked with perspiration, the owner paid me $75. I was so thankful. It felt good to actually produce something for our family. It has been a long time since my labor had generated a positive cash flow. I'll never forget that day or the feeling of satisfaction it brought.

September 27
I got another job this week hanging a sign ($50). Also, I was offered work painting trim for Stan Sizemore.

September 28
The Sizemore's gave us about $50 worth of beef!

I often noted my thoughts in my journal entries, but I never actually wrote with publication in mind. So my entries range from the mundane to the monetary to the majestic. I just wrote how things were for us in those early years. I imagined that one day my children or grandchildren might be blessed by watching God work. Some entries are lengthy. Below is a snippet from a lengthy entry illustrating the range, intensity, and variety of thoughts and issues racing through my mind on any given day.

November 11
Today... Prioritize time with God... Follow God into the streets today. Paint my signs and listen. Observe the people -- especially the poor. It may be that a mountain-man will come by... My children need me. I need to give them time... The Word is our comfort -- I must read it for reassurance and hope.

December 2
We are being carried by the gifts of others. Without them, I can safely say we would not still be in Appalachia. I wonder how much longer we can remain here unless either

the gifts increase or our earnings increase. The total of them is enough, but one or the other on their own would not be sufficient at this point. We're in a difficult stage of the journey -- doubts about the decision to be here are much more regular and convincing and yet, somehow, the Lord continues to empower and enable us to put one foot ahead of the next -- one day at a time.

The year 1996 closed with us living in our sweet little house on Florence Avenue. Many new faces, places, and experiences had been encountered. The children were healthy, and my mother had improved a good deal, though she still struggled with her pain.

[Stephen & Claudia Greek]

Stephen and Claudia Greek, our former coworkers in Kenya, had joined us during the year, and two other families we knew in Jellico were meeting with us for weekly worship. Our four families tried meeting in our homes on Wednesdays, even at the local clinic waiting room on Sundays, but the key to reaching Appalachian hearts remained elusive. However, by God's grace we remained, and with His continued grace, we would have more opportunities in the New Year. I concluded that He must want us here for some reason or we'd not have been sustained to this point.

16 months after leaving Kenya, steady employment remained a major concern. God had kept us supplied through the gifts and prayers of others, so we had survived financially, but it had not been as we'd expected. Being locally employed and working after hours to teach and encourage people toward God remained our vision, though in the next few months it would become unmistakably evident that God's vision and our initial vision were not exactly the same.

December 17

God has been great. Over the 1996 year, God has graciously given us almost $14,000.00.

1997 - DWANE P.

February 28
Today, I felt pretty low.

The sentiment of my February 28th entry continued. Near the end of March, I bottomed out.

Africa was difficult in its own ways -- malaria, threats of violence, cultural clashes, government instability -- but March in Appalachia holds its own room in my 'Museum of Low Moments.' Though God had provided for months, the constant 'what about tomorrow' was a grinding experience with a cumulative effect. I never knew what was beyond today except for bills. Though I probably should have, I had not yet learned to comfortably trust Him. My stomach stayed in a knot. In other words, "I worried." My worry was a sign that I had understood neither the greatness nor the nearness of God. I was still doubting… a double-minded man. If I had been more spiritually mature, I'd have found comfort and peace in Jesus' directive, "Don't worry about tomorrow."

In Exodus, Moses and God were talking like friends. Moses told God he'd like to know Him better, personally, by His Name. Knowing someone by name means knowing their character, their likes and dislikes, their mind and emotions. Moses was asking to know God's heart. Then a very interesting event occurred. God had Moses stand in a crevice in the stone face of the mountain and covered him with His hand. Then God stood with His back to Moses. Turning one's back is typically a sign of disfavor. Why does God turn His back toward this man in whom He just said that He found favor? On the surface, it seems inconsistent, but God's next words explain, "If you see my face, you will die." If I love someone, I will never purposefully harm them. There was something about seeing God, about knowing Him fully, that would have overwhelmed, even crushed Moses. A loving God wouldn't harm a man He truly cherished. So He protected him, "You can't see My face."

If you've never been present when an adult feels unconditionally loved for the first time, I'll tell you what happens -- they cry. They sob. Though it is a beautiful moment, it can get ugly -- tissues and tears and runny noses and the whole thing. Imagine such a breakdown multiplied a trillion times! A sudden and full experience of God's love would literally release more emotion than a person could manage. It could literally kill. So God shows Moses His back. He shows Moses the least, but most manageable, expression of His love (or the greatest expression of His rejection), which is still enough love for Moses to realize a deep, deep blessing throughout his lifetime. The intensity of God's love and the immediacy of His attentiveness toward us is more than can be expressed. He is VERY interested and concerned and involved in our daily lives -- especially when we are attempting to live according to His will and ways. He cannot forget our needs or us. Had I understood and believed this in 1997, I'd have enjoyed much greater personal peace. I had no reason to be concerned. I should have relaxed. We should all relax.

Think about it this way: most people arrive Monday morning and put in their forty hours till Friday. When the boss pays them at the end of the week, they don't sigh with relief, "Oh great! I am so thankful. I thought he might not pay me!" Other than looking forward to payday, there is seldom, if ever, any doubt about being paid. I mean, who would imagine an employee turning to his boss and with great relief saying, "OH! Thank you. I am so relieved. I was concerned you would not pay me this week!" Get the point? If an employee thought or said this, it would actually reveal the employee's distrust of his employer's integrity or ability. My worry was actually a very ugly case of distrust. I had not yet understood, or believed, or come to know the Name of this great loving God whose love for me is so intense that if I were to know it, I would be crushed by its intensity. Admittedly, I was not yet fully trusting Him. *(See the entry of 03/11/00 for evidence of growth in this area.)*

In the midst of all this internal wrestling, it had become clear that sign painting, like everything else I'd tried before it, was not going to meet our income needs. At the same time, local evangelism was stagnant. Casual friendships were growing in number, but meaningful inroads into the community were not. I saw overwhelming spiritual and social needs but had not connected with anyone ready for personal changes. Pinching pennies and seeking work consumed my time, energy, and attention. Almost daily I doubted the decision to move to Jellico, but I could not walk away because I was deeply convicted that God wanted to do something significant in Appalachia and that it involved us. It was this conviction that held my feet to the fire.

During March, though I was on the bottom, God was not far away. He never is -- *especially* when we are on the bottom. The next few entries demonstrate the unimaginable way in which He lifted us to new heights.

March 8

Several times in the past two weeks the words in John 14:27 have come to me. Twice it was during prayer that I thought, 'Peace I leave with you, my peace I give you. I do not give you as the world gives. Do not let your hearts be troubled, and do not be afraid.' I have found comfort in these verses.

March 30

Received an email from someone from Harding University (our college alma mater). Introduced himself as Dwane P. I looked him up in the yearbook. I vaguely recall him. He said he heard about our efforts in Appalachia through a mutual friend in Florida (Keith Williams). Dwane had been a vocational missionary in the Pacific Northwest and he wants to talk to me. I hope he has some insights into how to do vocational missions better. I can use the advice.

April 1
Today, I went to Knoxville to meet Dwane P....

The next entry in my journal is lengthy. I will summarize by saying that it explains how Dwane P. offered me a job on April 1st (no fooling)! It was a 'real job,' and one that I could operate from my home in Jellico! As he spoke with me that afternoon in Knoxville, I struggled to clearly understand the job he was offering. However, I did understand that Dwane P. applied godly principles in his business. This, of course, got my attention. He prayed at the conclusion of our meeting and then shocked me by offering to pay me $500 if I would invest 25 hours studying some video material about his field of business. After reviewing that material, if I wanted to proceed, he would hire me.

That $500 was the largest paycheck I'd earned in the nearly two years since our move to Appalachia. On my way home, through tears of joy and relief (and even of disbelief) running down my cheeks, I expressed my feelings to the LORD. As I said before, when a grown person realizes they are loved… it gets messy.

This event was so powerful, so meaningful, that I recorded it in full later in my 6/17/97 journal entry. A line from that entry reads,

Dwane's offer is one of those events that will certainly go down in our family-faith legacy as pivotal.

Dwane avoided taking loans to operate his business. He had only enough cash to guarantee me three months of work. If new business were generated during this time, he would offer me more. On the other hand, if after three months there were no 'sales,' he could promise nothing more.

I immediately got busy reviewing the videos and thereafter accepted the job on a commission basis of $1500 a month. Meanwhile, unsolicited gifts continued to fill the gaps in our budget. I dropped sign painting, MLM sales, and all my other work efforts and devoted myself exclusively to learning about information technology (IT) recruiting. Dwane's company, HTR, was in the business of recruiting information technology professionals and placing them in jobs fitting their skills and interests.

I'd been living in Africa while the computer industry had come of age. The height of my personal tech experience had been printing banners using a Commodore 64 computer on a dot-matrix printer. Technology had quickly developed its own culture and languages. It was an entirely new world for me, but language and culture were things I knew how to tackle. Soon enough I was spewing techno-terms and carrying on conversations about C++, Visual Basic, AS400, Cobol, Dbase, migrations, and operating platforms like I knew what they meant -- which I actually did not, though I knew how and when to use them in sentences. I guess you could say that the world of IT was my new jungle.

Dwane called June 30th 'the drop-dead deadline.' By June 30th I must either have landed an account or we would have to call it quits. He was honest with me and confessed, "My first placement in this business took 18 months." For a novice to make a placement in three months was a long, long-shot that most would have suggested might require an act of God.

Dwane was a great coach and very patient. God placed him in my path (he says God placed me in his path). This would prove true time and time again in ensuing years; however, at that season in our friendship, I needed to place someone in an IT job… and fast. The sand was racing through the hourglass.

Three months flew by quickly. On June 30th, the dawn's rays announced that the 'drop dead deadline' had arrived. I had made zero placements, but there was one in the works. After the sun had set that day, I made the following journal entry.

June 30

West S. with E-company (not the company name) called while I was interviewing a candidate for LS-Company (not the company name). Explaining to the candidate that I had to take the call, I listened in on the 3-way as West and Dwane discussed several issues regarding a candidate I'd earlier submitted to E-company for an AS400 position. They worked on several details and as the conversation wound to a conclusion... West accepted my candidate! My first placement!! I looked at my watch and the time was just after 4 p.m. Amazingly, the placement had come exactly three months, to the very hour, from the day I officially began working for Dwane. The deal landed Dwane's company double the amount he'd started with when he hired me which meant he could keep me employed for another six months! Praise the Lord.

Now about this point, you should expect that I'd have learned all the spiritual lessons I'd need about the whole income/work/mission thing -- right? Wrong. I still wrestled with doubt, but I wasn't the first. In Exodus God delivers more than ten miracles through Moses, including walking a dried seabed to safety, but three days later the folks are whining about wanting to go back! Jesus heals sick people, casts out demons, and turns a handful of bread into a gigantic banquet. Yet His buddies on the water with Him doubt the extent of His power when the waves pitch their boat. Learning that God shows up in one situation doesn't always translate into confidence in a new one. It should, but it doesn't; at least, until we learn that the differing situations shouldn't be our focus as much as the all-supreme sufficiency of Christ.

Unfortunately, less than six days after this exciting answer to prayer, I was wrestling with my thoughts and God's will again.

August 11

Rick & Sharon W. sent a totally unexpected check for $1000 today! They sent gifts earlier in the year of $350 and $1000. It... made me consider, 'Here I am working 50-60 hours per week for 1/3 of this amount. Should I rely on God 100% to supply our needs while I put 100% of my time into ministry?' These are times of confusion, questioning, a wandering in the wilderness. On the one hand, I am delighted to enjoy Dwane's friendship, while also receiving some steady income. On another hand, finding time to connect with local people remains a struggle. And what am I to do with the fact that, still, the majority of our income is from donations?

September 8
During the last approx. 4-5 weeks we have been given over $16,000 through gifts and earnings! This is almost too hard to believe.

December 15
The past two years have been difficult. Yet, looking back, there was actually no good reason to be fearful or stressed... God supplied our every need. God has shown Himself absolutely trustworthy. Not once did He turn His back on us.

[HTR Team   Dwane P. front center]

1998 - BUILDING THE HOUSE

January 3

The first gift of the New Year was $75 from Brian C. If God will be supplying all our needs through HTR, I'll inform our donors to discontinue their support, or at least I'll remind them that their giving should only be as God prompts them.

May 25

Rick & Sharon W. sold some stock and sent us all their profit! $604.27!

June 9

Someone paid our rent anonymously!

July 22

I am discouraged. My work at HTR has yet to be effective this year. I've had no placements in 1998. My house construction has only reached floor level and we still have no church. I wonder why I'm here sometimes.

When leaving Kenya, we sold all our personal items except a few things, which we intended to bring back in our suitcases. When our supporting church in

Tyler, Texas sent us to Kenya, they'd raised a large sum of money to set up our house and office in Kenya. We returned the cash from the sale of all those items to the church's mission account. Sales from our personal items were deposited in our personal savings account.

Our dream for many years was to have our own farm. Being very frugal while living in Africa allowed us to build up a modest savings. Though the first years in Appalachia nibbled into that savings, we invested some of it in a beautiful piece of farmland.

The Ballard family had reared a family on it before us, but as their health failed and children moved onto their own properties, they decided to sell the place and move to a more manageable situation. It was perfect for us, though there was no house on it.

We could not afford the whole property, so my friend and colleague, Steve Greek, and I bought it together and then divided it between us. After a year of clearing brush and clearing the property, we set to building our dream house.

To make owning our house a financial possibility, we determined to do it ourselves… literally. The idea energized me so much that, even under the crush of Mom's health crisis, our reverse culture shock issues, and the constant burden of provisions, we found time and energy to think, talk, and plan for a house.

I had no experience with or exposure to house building. The closest I'd come to construction was a very sad chicken coop I threw together in our first year of marriage. Donna remembered my first attempt at construction too, and it made her 'nervous' as she pondered the prospects that I was seriously considering building our house! However, I convinced her I could and would do a better job this time. She trusted me, and off we went!

I remember walking heel-to-toe across the Florence Avenue house's kitchen to estimate its length and width. I would then ask Donna if she wanted a kitchen that was longer, wider, or smaller. If she wanted something a little wider I added a few steps until it felt right for her. From there I drew 'blueprints' using a 12" plastic ruler and a sheet of notebook paper. I drafted plans for the entire house that way. I asked a friend in Texas to help with the attic drawings since the roof's dimensions would not be so straightforward. My Texas friend was a draftsman and would know how I could get the most from that space. Of course, drawings were the easy part; there was a steep and long learning curve ahead of us. For one thing, we didn't realize how a few decisions at the beginning would affect the size of our place. The choice to add a basement and then to make rooms in the attic added a LOT of floor space (and cost). For example, one simple misunderstanding cost me a very large amount of money and a good year of extra work.

I dove into books on carpentry, and they helped, but the personal advice of those experienced with laying footers, framing, roofing, wiring, plumbing, etc. gave me the most practical information, though their advice sometimes conflicted. Learning came at a price... especially when the classroom was the School of Hard Knocks.

Still, I was able to know my options and avoid many mistakes. I learned quickly, yet every step seemed to be agonizingly s-l-o-w. Many friends, neighbors, and even strangers helped for a few hours or a few days during those months and years of construction. Even in this, God was nudging people to our aid. Our three-plus year building process was not as fast as Nehemiah's 52-day reconstruction project, but it was something of a first cousin. In both cases, the people worked enthusiastically as if serving the Lord Himself.

My two older sons, Daniel and Caleb, were 12 and 10 when we began. They worked like grown men the entire time. Sometimes it was so hot we could only last an hour before we had to rehydrate with slugs of fresh water from our spring. I say "slugs" because I would send one of the boys to the spring to fill a two-liter bottle and literally quaff the whole thing down in one long, deep 'slug.' My young sons were amazing, and I could not have done the work without them. All the family helped in one way or another. One late October night, after a Wednesday worship meeting, our kids spent the night bundled up in our car. While Daniel, Caleb, Hannah, and Benjamin slept, Donna and

I laid a section of floor that needed to be completed before daylight. She held a light for me as I lay flooring. We started at 9 p.m. and worked the entire night. Heavy fog turned to thin ice under our feet around 3 a.m. At 8 a.m. the framers pulled to a stop in our drive as we literally drove the last nail.

My children never complained even once. They were amazing little troopers throughout the entire project, and I cannot say enough about how eager and willing they were to be a part. I think this too was a serendipitous gift from God. Those hard, hot hours together bonded us so that throughout their teen years and into their adulthood we communicated well and still can work together. We might have missed that gift under any other circumstances. We credit God for His wonderful ability to wring value from the driest situation.

Pretty early on in our building journey, it became clear that I had bitten off more than I could chew, but there was no backing out. In fact, we had no options. We didn't have enough savings to purchase a house outright, I would not shackle myself or my family with a bank loan, renting would eventually deplete our funds in a few years with nothing to show for it, and I was convinced I could build our house for $25 a square foot. Doing it ourselves seemed the best route for us. Though I often questioned both my decision and my abilities, I forged ahead.

When the roof was on I focused on the rooms for my mom in a small apartment connected to the main house and some sleeping quarters, a bathroom, and a small kitchen in the basement where we would live once these were functional. In 1999, we left the Florence house, but it was another two years before the upstairs bedrooms were completed and another two years before the main floor was finished. It's been 18 years now, and there are still unfinished areas, but the house is beautiful and functions very nicely.

Dwane P. and I were reflecting just a few days ago, and he said, "Steve, I often wonder how you did it." I wonder too. The strength came from God's hand during the building process and throughout the years since. I safely estimate that we've hosted over 3000 people in our home over the years; many of them being overnight(s). Donna has served truckloads of food, my children have washed mountains of dishes, and floor space has been over night sleeping space for teens and adult guests from around the world. Our visitors, whether individuals, groups, families, friends or those seeking answers for life, have blessed us more than we've blessed them.

[Daniel & Caleb helping build]

Due to our building experience, my sons now know how to work hard and, of course, build; Donna and I have fond memories like the all-nighter in the freezing temps -- though, thankfully, the kids don't remember sleeping in the car; my children easily welcome guests, know how to wash dishes, clean house, and make work fun. They know how to entertain themselves with sticks, rocks, string, wood, leaves, and insects or 'critters' instead of electronic gadgets. In addition, because we talked to each other on the job site and while preparing for guests, our children got to know their mother and me, and we got to know them. They've heard true stories of faith and struggle. They've also brushed shoulders with those still in the midst of drug abuse, alcoholism, and relationship tensions. Though there were struggles in those years, there were blessings that made them worthwhile. At some point, even the financial gains began to outweigh the costs. As of 2013, the cost of our home construction came to about $29 a square foot -- which is quite amazing; and this included the cost of our 33 acres! The only 'loss' is that my right elbow now creeks and pops sometimes -- I've diagnosed it as 'hammer-elbow.'

In 1998 these good times were still a dream. The reality at that time was that, though two local physicians were heroic in the extra measures they took to find Mom a helpful treatment, and though she was beginning to function a bit better and could sleep without the twitching, she still suffered. This meant better sleep for me since I no longer needed to sleep in the chair by her bed. The doctor's newly designed regimen of medications even enabled her to watch the kids if we needed to step out to the store for a few minutes. I can never thank Dr. Frank Agnoli or Dr. Bruce Woodall enough for taking extra measures in her care. Saying that God helped us doesn't mean it was easy, and some of my journal entries revealed the strain. Meanwhile, I was working full-time for Dwane P. and trying to start a local church. The little sleep I got was sound but did not totally replenish me. I felt tired all the time. The church planting effort was discouraging, but something in my heart would not release me from plodding on. By God's grace, we continued.

August 5

Jim A., a member of Mid-Cities Church in Colleyville, Texas, heard about our ministry and, because they were looking to add some additional mission work, called today and asked if they could be a part of ours! They'll be sending $200 monthly for one year!

At breakfast this morning we had read 2 Chronicles 20, where King Jehoshaphat's famous statement is recorded: "For we have no power to face this vast army that is attacking us. We do not know what to do, but our eyes are upon You." Later the king's army marches out to discover their enemy has been defeated and the army's work was only to collect the plunder. Today we have seen that the Lord still delivers plunder without us lifting a finger -- except to receive it. Oh, how good the favor of the Lord is. How blessed it is to have His attention. How kind and gracious is the LORD, who sends blessings down from heaven -- gifts in just the right measure. Praise the LORD. Forever, praise His Holy Name.

September 5

K.I.M. gave us $500. She is a poor lady but always teaches

me rich lessons. I am humbled, and my first reaction was to decline, but it is pride that would have done that. I must receive from the Lord, and she must follow His nudges. Praise Him. May He bless her.

October 28
God is full of surprises.

November 5
I've been reviewing our financial position... completing the house with the money we have left will be very close. However, I also sense that this is simply a last minute trial. I've been tempted to take a loan -- a close friend also recommended that I should get one -- but I do not have peace about it. I think I will persevere a while longer and look to the Lord to provide. I don't think a loan has any spiritual value or lacks any spiritual value, but for myself, I do not have God's peace about it. Instead, I believe I should rely upon Him fully for these provisions. God hasn't failed us yet, and it would strengthen the testimony if He supplied completely.

In the end, we completed the house without a loan, and I believe the resulting testimony is more inspiring than if we'd turned to men for our supplies.

December 10
John M. Family sent a gift of $2000! Praise the Lord! Great timing!

December 15
• Dwane P. gave each employee a $500 year-end gift.
• An anonymous family paid our rent again. This is a total of $1200 for the year from whoever is paying rent for us. We are humbled.

December 31

This year, through friends, churches, family, and work at HTR, the Lord has supplied $38,344.86! In addition, there were a number of non-cash items given for our use.

1998 closed with us juggling the construction of a house, work at HTR, and the effort to launch an indigenous Appalachian church. It was a difficult year for Dwane's company. He taught me much about business, and about the Lord. We had become very close friends, but the financial successes of our first six months did not continue. There was no new business on my part for the whole of 1998. A constant tug-of-war raged in me as I struggled over whether or not to continue with HTR.

Still, God had managed to provide for us for another year. We entered the new millennium still living in the Florence Avenue house, but 1999 would change that and more.

1999 - FOUNDING GOODSOIL

January 31

I have not had a placement with HTR for fourteen months. I do not know what to change, or how to improve or enhance the outcome of my work.

I had Bible study and prayer with Donny L. last week. He is not responding, yet.

February 8

Our children were invited to a local event today. Part of the fun included lunch at the local pizzeria. Because our income was so low, we quietly decided against sending our kids; however, a perceptive friend apparently suspected why we weren't allowing them to go and offered to buy pizza today. Of course, we were delighted that our children could now participate, but the offer struck my personal pride. Whether dealing with wealth or poverty, it is difficult to check one's pride properly. It is difficult to be in the position of having little, and it is humbling to receive. My pride is probably the reason we've been chosen for financial dependence on God. During our decade in Kenya, we were the comparatively affluent ones and able to financially assist those with less, but I must confess that with the shoe now on the other foot, I've had my eyes opened. I'm ashamed to admit that I sometimes scolded the Africans for mismanagement and gave to them begrudgingly. I'm sure my lectures, rather than instructing or benefiting them, served rather to embarrass and humiliate. Lord, forgive me and bless this dear friend who has given to us today with generosity *and* grace.

February 25
I completed an application for work at a Wal-Mart distribution center in London, KY. I spoke to Dan G. about carpentry work. He said he could pay me $7 per hour. I can also stack rocks at Ketchum's Stone Quarry for extra money. The quarry work is my least favorite choice, but still an option. We have again been reduced financially to ground zero... or very near it. The Lord reigns. I believe it; I truly do.

March 1
Mr. and Mrs. E. sent Donna $25 "for her own personal use." The Lord is so thoughtful to be watching out for my bride. We are also able to send Glenn R. family a gift for mission work in Atlanta. We are also sending Larry C. family a gift for missions in East Africa. Both gifts are sent by faith in these more-lean-than-usual-times. We believe that we should share from our provisions, no matter how large or small, as a further show of trust in God. Our eyes are on Him.

God's divine principle of giving never has limits or exclusions. We give when we have much, and we give when we have little. Giving yields blessings. Farmers who hoard seed are unwise. They must 'tithe' a portion by reinvesting it in the soil if they expect a harvest. We are neither an exception to this principle of sowing nor do we expect we will be exempt from its produce.

"Remember this: Whoever sows sparingly will also reap sparingly, and whoever sows generously will also reap generously. Each man should give what he has decided in his heart to give, not reluctantly or under compulsion, for God loves a cheerful giver. And God is able to make all grace abound to you, so that in all things at all times, having all that you need, you will abound in every good work... Now he who supplies seed to the sower and bread for food will also supply and increase your store of seed and will enlarge the harvest of your righteousness. You will be made rich in every way so that you can be generous on every occasion, and through us, your generosity will result in thanksgiving to God" (2 Corinthians 9:6-12).

A memorable example of this principle occurred several years before, while we were still living in Kenya, when we learned of a medical need of a friend of an acquaintance. The expense of their procedure was great, and we felt nudged by the LORD to contribute. I remember hesitating at first, possibly giving a smaller amount, but together we decided on a number quite a bit greater than we normally give, but we both had peace about it. We sent $700.00.

Just a few weeks later, our seed came back as a harvest when we received a totally unexpected surprise gift of a whopping $7000.00! Exactly ten times what we had given! God cannot be out-given. His delight is to be generous, but He can only add to an empty vessel.

March 3
I woke this morning with so many ideas for ministry!

March 5
Today, I reconsidered many issues. One was my purpose here and what I'm doing about it. Life is really short and the needs are enormous. I asked myself, "What am I doing in that office every day from morning until evening?" My reply was, "I'm providing *some* income for my family -- which is

honorable -- but I'm also not out with people. My heart is pounding louder every day to get on with our original purpose for our being here! I am certain that people would respond, and I know they need Jesus -- everyone does."

On a memorable day in April, two years after first meeting Dwane and accepting his offer to join HTR, I drove to Nashville to meet with him. He had contacted me for that initial meeting; I asked him for this one.

The three-hour drive seemed much longer than usual. I began our meeting by expressing my sincere gratitude for all he and his family had done for me and for my family. The speech I'd rehearsed a dozen times that morning began to spill out as I explained that since I was not producing a benefit to HTR's bottom line, I did not feel it was fitting for me to continue to drain the company. In keeping with his selfless spirit, Dwane offered to keep me on by cutting his own income in half! Such pure selflessness is rare in life and even more so in business. If Dwane's model of business were ever to become the practice of business in America, there would be no more need for picket lines, labor laws, or union organizing, and we'd all be better off as a society for following this standard of love.

We had both made the right decisions -- I to remove myself to benefit the company and him to reduce his benefits to retain the employee. Our motivation was identical -- a genuine concern for the good of the other. We knew without a doubt that we were in the presence of the proverbial 'friend that is closer than a brother.' It may not be a 'manish' thing to admit, but we both cried. It was David and Jonathan.

The income from HTR had been a wonderful gift, and the business and management education I'd gotten had equipped me for my future. God had timed Dwane's arrival with my lowest moment and used HTR to fund and encourage our ministry for an additional two years.

Dwane and I had both hoped HTR income would grow until only ten hours a week were necessary for work with the balance of our time available for local ministry. Though our business aspirations were not realized, we had been enabled to remain in Appalachia, and what I had learned from Dwane (and what he had learned from me) would prove profitable.

Fast-forwarding a decade, it is interesting how God continued to work within our two families. In 2002, fully 'infected' with the missions bug, Dwane and his family closed HTR and begin a church-planting mission in Germany. A few years later, Donna and I traveled to their home in Leipzig. While with them, Dwane took us to Halle, Germany, where we saw the Francke Foundation. It is the site of the orphanage and school (1700s) where George Müller's vision and passion for orphans and trust in God's provisions got their start. For me, it was like visiting an ancestral homeland, a touch with some original root that reached into my own life's story.

Dwane's family invested five years in Leipzig, returning to the USA only reluctantly due to circumstances beyond their control. He and his oldest daughters have returned for short visits on several occasions. In 2011 their oldest daughter (who is currently living in Germany) launched a ministry to young girls in rural Arkansas, and in 2014 their second daughter joined a mission team in Mozambique. Truly, by Divine design, the outcomes of our few years together in HTR had not only met Dwane's and my expectations... they exceeded them.

Within three days of leaving HTR, I found a local job in construction. The company owner, Dan G., hired me as a laborer. Though I'd built my own house, I had no formal construction experience. My first duties for Dan involved keeping the job site as clean and orderly as possible, which meant that I swept, hauled trash, and followed the carpenters removing debris.

One 'skill' that I did possess was painting. After cleaning the construction area, I used a brush to 'cut in' the corners and hard-to-reach areas ahead of the professional painters. I painted wall joints and corners and around doors and windows. I didn't mind the work. In fact, it was a welcome change from the stressful requirements of recruiting I'd faced daily at HTR. There was a trade-off, however. Unlike the mature, thoughtful, humble Dwane, my immediate 'supervisor' on the construction site was a twenty-year-old who had a condescending attitude. Within minutes of my first day there, I knew he could either be a challenge or an opportunity. I think he decided he would be a challenge, but I decided that he would be an opportunity.

Making only $7 an hour, the $1.70 per gallon cost of fuel to and from work chewed into my meager take-home pay. To compensate, I limited lunch breaks to 15 minutes and worked straight through breaks the other workers took for smoking or coffee. Every minute counted and I needed every dime.

The afternoon of my third day Dan pulled me aside, "I've seen how you work, Steve. What would it take to get you on full time?" We talked and he increased my wages from $7 an hour to $10 -- matching my HTR base salary. In just three days God had restored our income fully!

This wasn't the only promotion Dan would offer. Eight weeks later he made me the head of one of three divisions in his company, which made me responsible for taking a house from the ground to the roof. My guys and I transferred blueprint measurements into a concrete footer, framed walls, set trusses, and a completed roof. It was heavy, hot, bruising work, but it was rewarding to see drawings become reality. Dan increased my wages again to $11.50 an hour and reimbursement for my fuel though I never asked for an increase or complained about my wages. Dan was a good man whose heart easily responded to God's nudges.

While working for Dan I learned that construction involved four basic elements: concrete, metal, wood, and sweat. We spent ten to twelve hours many days in the open sun. Concrete waits for no one, and when pouring a footer or a wall, we could not stop just because our watches indicated it was quitting time. We pushed through on concrete projects until they were completed. One particularly hot and demanding day, three of the four men on my crew suffered mild heatstroke in our effort to complete a footer despite weather conditions.

Construction was demanding physically, but more than that, it was also requiring almost all of my time. Leaving home at 5 a.m., returning at 6 p.m., and then rushing out again to work on my own house until as late as 10 p.m. left me physically exhausted and mentally dazed some evenings. I was either building Dan's houses or my own 6 ½ days and nights of the week. My body and mind screamed in complaint that they would not be pushed at that pace indefinitely.

There were memorable redeeming aspects of those months. Over the weeks, my crew and I became friends, and it wasn't too long before we started our days circled up at the job site, praying before working. One afternoon, that challenging young supervisor (now under my authority) and I were shoveling out a ditch together after heavy storms had caused a section of footer to cave in. I don't recall what led us to the conversation -- men don't always chit-chat on the job, but he suddenly spoke. "There! You can bury those." Between us, on the ground, lay a pack of cigarettes he'd thrown down. I asked what he meant. He said, "I'm done with them. I want to change." So, we prayed -- telling God the young man's desire to stop smoking and be changed. When our prayer concluded, the young man said, "Amen," and we returned to our digging.

Over the next half-year, there were several deep and sometimes tearful conversations with the men on my crew. Smoke breaks converted into conversations about being better dads and better husbands. My men were being changed, but the path to reaching Appalachia would not pass through them. They were followers, like Andrew. We needed 'Peters' and 'Pauls.'

As summer gave way to fall, I explored the requirements to establish a non-profit organization through which we could invest in local and international missions. After consulting with our coworkers, the Greeks, we identified three areas where we believed we should be involved: Appalachian church planting, the training of young people who were interested in missions, and service to missionaries and their families. It was still unclear exactly how or when I was to proceed into these, but the physical and emotional drain on me as Dan's employee was reaching deeper into my reserves. I was able to relate more to Paul's words in 2 Corinthians 1:9-11:

"Indeed, in our hearts, we felt the sentence of death. But this happened that we might not rely on ourselves, but on God, who raises the dead. He has delivered us from such a deadly peril, and he will deliver us. On him, we have set our hope that he will continue to deliver us, as you help us by your prayers. Then many will give thanks on our behalf for the gracious favor granted us in answer to the prayers of many."

It was six more months before I would discern the direction we should take.

March 11
I learned I'll need between $500-$1000 to register a non-profit organization. This is a top-level prayer request beginning now.

It was on March 11th, 1999 that I prayed, "LORD, we need between $500 and $1000 from sources, or in ways, that will help me discern if you would have us establish a non-profit for mission purposes."

March 15
This morning was snowy. Steve G. was homebound so I asked him to come and pray... I shared my Mission Camp thoughts with him... A check arrived today from an anonymous donor for $470.00. Is this the money for the N.P.O. registration? Is it the first fruits for the Mission Camps?

March 16
A gift today from Mr. & Mrs. E. for $25 and another from Bernice W. for $50.00 came today. Bernice offered to be a prayer team member!

March 17
Shocked today when I received gift of $300 from Peggy W.! This is the first time she has ever made a donation. Her gift included a note: "Use it as you see best." This gift brings the last three days' total to $845 for 'general uses.' $845 is somewhere between $500-$1000! I'm

supposing that these are God's go-ahead for the founding of a non-profit for missions!

I called a friend who is experienced with drawing up the documents needed for registration of non-profit organizations. She told me she would do it for $200. I told her, "We have that much, let's get started."

GoodSoil Ministries Inc. was officially founded five months later, in October. During the process, fees and other costs were incurred. They are itemized below so you may do the math yourself and rejoice in awe at God's exactitude, and so also that you may understand why we were completely affirmed in the establishment of GoodSoil Ministries.

Fee to lady who helped with Non-Profit process	$200
Federal Registration	$500
State Registration	$100
Name Reservation fee	$20
Stamps, Phone calls, fuel	$25
Total Cost	**$845**

God had answered our prayer of "somewhere between $500 and $1000," and He had confirmed our direction with exactitude.

Though we would be the first to caution anyone not to assume that adequate financing of a project is infallible evidence of God's approval, we nonetheless took these gifts, along with all the other signs of His provision, as confirmation that our decision had God's support. We were greatly energized.

March 25
I asked the Lord to send $15k-$20k so we could quickly finish the house and have more time for ministry.

March 27
Miraculous! -- God sent $5000 via the Goodman family along

with a note on which was written Psalm 20:1-5. This affirms us, and more than anything it lets me know, again, that God, who made everything, hears my prayers.

Psalm 20:1-5
May the LORD answer you when you are in distress;
may the name of the God of Jacob protect you.
May he send you help from the sanctuary
and grant you support from Zion.
May he remember all your sacrifices
and accept your burnt offerings.
May he give you the desire of your heart
and make all your plans succeed.
May we shout for joy over your victory
and lift up our banners in the name of our God.
May the LORD grant all your requests.

A word here about my use of the term 'miraculous.' A good friend cautioned me sometime later about calling our prayer answers miraculous. I appreciate his word of caution, and would never wish to over-reach in expressing my view of this or other prayer answers, but I struggle with a more accurate term. I believe that manna from the thin air of heaven is a miracle, as is the multiplication of a few loaves to feed a multitude and the transformation of water into wine. The exact coinage from a fish's mouth to pay tribute and words from a donkey are as well. So, is the overhearing of a plot by a young boy to save Paul's life equal to the earthquake that broke him out of jail? Is the offer of Joseph of Arimathea to take Jesus' body to his sepulcher less an intervention of God than the moving of the stone from its entrance days later? Is it less a miracle when God involves a widow's oil and flour than when He simply rains food from the sky? I get confused about drawing lines in these matters, and there may be differences between them, but I see a common element: God's involvement in them. Perhaps 'miracle' is too strong. I don't have any problem hearing that, and therefore none of what I have experienced these 20+ years may technically be a miracle. This doesn't shake my faith in the least. What to label all that has happened is not really as important as the fact that they happened when and how they did. Something unusual happened over and over and over again. The degree and specificity of so many requests and answers suggest God's involvement in them. So, while I agree that they may not rank as miracles on the order of dividing the Red Sea or raising the dead, I struggle very much to call them 'accidents,' 'coincidence,' or even 'ordinary.' They are extra-ordinary, and I believe most will agree with me that there is strong supporting evidence that God hears and responds when we call on Him.

May 20
Dan G. promoted me again and increased my wages from $10 per hour (approx. $20,000 annually) to $24,000 annually plus profit sharing. He also offered to pay for my fuel. God alone knows the reasons for this promotion from $7 per hour as a floor sweeper about 8 weeks ago to a full salary and a divisional leadership role. The story of Joseph does come to my mind.

The summer was extremely hot, yet I was given the energy to manage an incredible schedule. However, as exciting as the promotions within Dan's company were, the job was consuming my life. I was working 10-12 hours a day for him, then in the evenings and into the night on my own house. By mid-August it was clear that I couldn't physically continue both for long. Yet I urgently needed to dry-in my own house before winter. Working on both construction projects left little time (or energy) for ministry or family. My prayers for guidance intensified.

Since those days, I have learned a lesson that would have helped me during that season of intense strain and stress. Specifically, I've learned the Hebrew meanings of two important words: 'stress' and 'thorn bush.'

I have come to understand that Hebrew letters are pictographic. Hebrew letters are more sketches of ideas, and Hebrew words are like stories being told one letter/thought at a time. For example, the word for "thorn bush" is *qots.*

Qof: ק is the first symbol/letter of the word *qots*. *Qof* represents holiness. Certain bowls, forks, spoons, etc. used in the Temple had a ק stamped on them to indicate that they were set apart for special purposes -- they were holy. As you can see, the letter *qof* looks like a spoon or ladle. The second letter in thorn bush is *vav:* ו. *Vav* resembles the profile of a person standing with a head at the top and body extending to the ground. *Vav* is the letter representing man or mankind.

The last letter in the word for thorn bush is *tzaddi:* צ. This letter has more than one meaning, but the one I'll emphasize is 'righteousness.' This letter *tzaddi* is made of two strokes, which are actually two other Hebrew letters or characters. The first is *nun:* נ, and it resembles the image of a man (a *vav*) on his knees. *Nun* pictures humility. The other letter used to make a *tzaddi* is the character *yod:* י. *Yod* depicts the Spirit of God and resembles a hand up in the sky. In *tzaddi* we see a man kneeling beneath the hand of God. Thus, *tzaddi* is the picture of one who humbles himself under the hand/Spirit of God -- a righteous man. Interestingly, *tzaddi* was also said to resemble a fishhook. A fishhook transports a fish from one place of existence (water) to another (air). It is in humbling ourselves before God that we are transported from carnal living into spiritual living. You can see how Peter, James, and Paul likely drew on these concepts when instructing the early church.[4]

• "Humble yourselves, therefore, under God's mighty hand, that he may lift you up in due time." -1 Peter 5:6
• "Humble yourselves before the Lord, and he will lift you up." -James 4:10
• "And so he condemned sin in sinful man, in order that the **righteous** requirements of the law might be fully met in us, who do not live according to **the sinful nature** but according to **the Spirit**." -Romans 8:3-4

When a person is set apart for God (holy) they allow the Spirit of God to lead, guide, and direct them. When things are easy, submission to God is easy,

---

4 For more delightful insights into the Hebrew alphabet I recommend L. Grant Luton's *In His Own Words*, Beth Tikkun Publishing.

but when times of **trouble**, **tribulation**, and **hardship** are experienced, the question is whether or not the "holy man" will continue to submit to the ways and will of God. We consider the person who continues to yield to God's Spirit, in spite of **pain** (thorn bushes), to be a truly righteous person.

Humility is part of righteousness, but so is faithful endurance through suffering. The first mention of pain in Scripture is in Genesis, and we see that there it is connected with the thorn bush.

*"Cursed is the ground because of you; through **painful** toil you will eat of it all the days of your life. It will produce **thorns** and thistles for you… by the sweat of your **brow** you will eat your food…" -Genesis 3:17-19*

The painful prick of the thorn bush is associated with the rebellion of the first man, Adam. In contrast, the second Adam, Jesus, the righteous man, is crowned with thorns. Hanging on the cross, Jesus embodied steadfastness to the will and ways of God in the midst of trial and testing; through them He became our righteousness.

Difficulties, trials, and tribulation are what test us to see if we will be unrighteous like the first Adam or righteous like the second Adam. Paul encouraged, "Our light and momentary troubles are achieving for us an eternal glory that far outweighs them all." James says, "Consider it pure joy when you face trials… don't you know that the testing of your faith produces perseverance, and perseverance must finish its work so that you may be mature?" John assures, "Do not be afraid of what you are about to suffer. Be faithful even unto death, and I will give you the crown of life." I wish I'd understood these truths when I was pushing through those long days and nights of our first years in Appalachia. I think I'd have weathered them more appreciatively knowing that there was Divine purpose behind them and the seed of personal spiritual benefit within them.

August 17
I was called a few days ago and asked to interview for a job at Cumberland College (a Christian college 15 minutes

away). I scheduled and attended the interview. I can do the job, and it would mean a steady income, but the position, like the one I'm in now, would demand almost all of my time (even Saturdays). I can't do it, start a church, AND work on a mission camp for training teens. The position's time commitment is so great that I don't truly believe I could invest in my family or ministry adequately. I'll seek the counsel of wise men and then decide.

I did seek wise counsel, and the conversations were interesting. First, I shared the situation with Mike Y. After sharing the whole story, I asked him, "Which job do I take? Do I stay with Dan or take the university position?" He answered without hesitation. "Well, I don't know if I could do it, but I think you should just go on and do what the LORD sent you up there to do." If I understood him correctly, he was saying that he didn't think he could drop his current sources of income and step into an unfunded ministry... but he thought that I should! I appreciated his candid honesty. His advice sounded like it was probably the right thing to do, but I did what I would advise anyone else to do -- I got a second opinion. I called my old friend Dwane P. Dwane listened also. I did not tell him Mike's response, but when I asked his thoughts, his answer stunned me. Almost word-for-word, Dwane repeated what Mike had said! I thanked him and sat back to absorb what I'd just heard. Two brothers, independent of each other, had just advised me to go from a position of employment and steady income to one of trusting in God to provide through sources and in manners of His choosing. I then did what any faith-filled believer would do -- I got a third opinion! Mark B. is a wise and trusted brother. He listened to the story and concurred with the advice of Mike and Dwane, adding that his own son is a missionary and that this was not the direction he would suggest for his son, yet he sensed keenly that it was appropriate for Donna and me. Wisdom was at work, yet this was so personally challenging, and the stakes so high, that I felt I needed to hear from one more source.

Donna and I decided to run the entire scenario by our good friends and coworkers, the Greeks. We explained to them the situation -- sharing what

Mike, Dwane, and Mark had suggested. When a few of their questions were answered, their thoughts concurred with the others!

Donna and I knew that this had been difficult advice for our friends to offer -- each readily admitting it wasn't something they were ready to do themselves -- but sensing strongly that we should follow what appeared to be God's leading.

Their agreement helped me gulp hard and move forward into what I had detected for months to be God's desired direction for us. In addition to all of this, it is important to add that in spite of my resistance, Donna had been encouraging me in this direction for at least four months before I took it to these friends and advisors! "Husbands, listen to your wives," rang in my ears.

The following Monday morning, as recorded in the journal entries below, I submitted my two weeks' notice to Dan G. We were at the end of a project, so he did not require me to complete the two weeks.

August 18
Dwane P. suggested I go full-time into ministry. He said, "Mark it down." So, I have.

August 23
I informed Dan G on Monday that I'm moving into full-time ministry.

August 25
Today begins my first day of full-time ministry. I told no one about our support situation (or lack of it), but at our study tonight David & Mary B. inquired about our support situation! I merely replied, "It is a faith mission."

September 3
Today, God sent the first 'official' gift to GoodSoil Ministries. Dwane and Molly P. gave $1500. This was a

generous sacrifice of faith for them. They also informed us that they would be sending $200 per month. They are rare and faithful friends.

September 4
Brian C. sent $50 to GoodSoil. I will open an account with this and Dwane and Molly's donation.

September 7
Mike Y. called to donate a couch and filing cabinets.

Mike's filing cabinets are still in use by GoodSoil, and the couch received spills, rips, tears, and the imprints of lots of tiny feet; hosted conversations, prayers, and fellowship between us and thousands of guests; and bore witness to the petitions and celebrations of thousands of prayers until, threadbare, it was replaced in the spring of 2017.

September 13
An accounting of our funds shows we will have a balance of $670 in our personal checking and $120 in the GoodSoil account after paying rent and outstanding bills. Our monthly expenses are typically $2500-$3000. I am willing to withdraw our savings, but I am hesitant. My sense is that God prefers to rescue me instead of me rescuing myself. There is an opportunity here for God to assure me of His involvement in this time of my life and ministry and to bring honor and glory to Himself along with increased faith to those who will someday read or hear of this day.

September 15
I am fasting today due to our financial circumstances. Sometimes fasting is easy -- today it is not. I am nauseous. Discerning the specific will of God is a challenging theological matter and has been hashed and rehashed since and before the time of Christ. So it is important to understand that I am not purporting that my understanding

of God's ways is flawlessly accurate. Rather, I am candidly sharing my journey with regard to my understanding of God. Either way, throughout the course of these 20 years it seems that God has been willing to work with my understandings -- accurate or not so accurate. I have concluded that God is greater than the accuracy of our understanding and that His chief concern is the direction of our heart. This does not mean that He cares nothing for truth and understanding, but that He cares most about humility. Certainly, Donna and I have been pure in our desire to please and obey Him.

Also, today we began a weekly noontime prayer with three other people from the Wesleyan church. We are asking for God to cause a local revival. I think the Enemy would like it if we were distracted from our focus on that event. However, I am aware that this 'test' is, in fact, an opportunity to grow in my resolve for this ministry and in reliance upon God.

Tonight, at prayer meeting, I felt I should see Donny L. I had prayed earnestly two days ago for his salvation. I planned to read Acts 2:35-42 with him and encourage him to obey Christ and be immersed for the removal of his sins. He wasn't home, so I left him a note. Around 11 p.m. he called. He had not yet read the note, but asked if I would baptize him this Sunday!

September 19
Donny L. was immersed today! We have scheduled a weekly Bible study with him and his wife beginning tomorrow at 7 p.m. God, Thank You.

September 20
Received gift from Mid-Cities church -- $450.

September 21
David and Mary B. sent $500 gift today and pledged monthly

support of $200. We cried. Their gift touched us in a way that few have -- I don't know why. (See 8/25/99.)

Received a gift from Texas George and family for $150. Looks like I will withdraw our IRA savings without a penalty so I can pay for what it takes to dry-in the house and we can move in.

September 23
We sent a gift of $500 to a Knoxville missionary -- Mrs. Anna Mae D.

If it seems odd that we would withdraw from our savings one day and then give away half a grand only a few days later, it isn't surprising. There is a simple explanation. We believe that we should be the first to give. I mean not only to give of our time and energy but also to give of our financial means. With that understood, in this case, we did not donate to the Knoxville missionary out of our savings. We were giving out of money we'd earned or been given over the time leading up to this entry on September 23.

As for how much to give, I will not set a figure. I don't operate by a figure myself. I do have some guidelines I use. Whether they are of the LORD is for each to decide. Our guide is to give 10% of all we receive (yes, before taxes, etc.). We sometimes give beyond this in response to occasional opportunities or what we call 'nudges' from the LORD. We have NEVER been able to out give Him when doing so out of a pure and thankful heart.

September 24
I am thrilled by the thoughts God brought me this morning during prayer. He helped me see that I have been called into a wonderful position. It is as if God is blessing me as He did the Levite, the Prophet, and the King. What I mean is that He is calling me into His divine service and making provision for me in that work. My 'job' is to be ready to do His work. My obligation is to wait upon Him,

His things, His timing. I suppose I could be compared to
a waiter or page. I can't describe it well; however, I
believe that I now have a clearer understanding that my
position is of one who ministers/serves before the LORD.
I'm to be present before Him and attentive to His wishes.
In a real sense, I have the privilege of standing in God's
presence! He wants me near Him, to rely upon Him, to
listen to His voice, to quickly carry out His requests.
Wow! This is such an honor. I hope I do not disappoint Him.

Here I must pause. Over fifteen years have passed since I wrote those thoughts.
This very morning (10/28/14), as I presented myself before the LORD and
then listened for His voice, I recognized that I have procrastinated too long
in preparing this testimony, which is an example of how one can neglect a
Divine appointment.

I believe that arrangements, intended by God for some special need or
occasion, can be missed. We can drop the ball. It has been this way from the
beginning of humanity, when there were myriads of blessings God had in
store for Adam, but due to his failings, they were not all realized. God had
great dreams for Samson, but he continually followed his own timetable,
his own interests, and his own means. The pages of Scripture drip with the
tears of regret and sorrow for missed God-appointments (Saul before the
Philistines; Israel wandering 40 years; "Jerusalem, Jerusalem!... How often
I would have...") I recognize my personal failures to act in step with divine
urgency. My failings cannot be undone. At some things I can never take a
second swing. We are not given another chance to accomplish or experience
once-in-a-lifetime opportunities. Knowing this would be a great burden and
depressing except for the fact that God is able to make beauty from ashes.
What I have spoiled is sadly lost to me; but in some other way God is still able
to accomplish something good, bestow a kindness, and redeem the time. I do
not claim to understand all of this, only to be a witness to the truth of it.

We have started praying for land for Missions Camps. I was
told of 250 acres on Capuchin Mountain. I think I will

drive out to see it and pray there today.

Also, the thought of a missionary recovery ministry is stirring my heart. I didn't have an immediate affinity for the idea, but recently, and especially today in prayer, I was struck with how much healing and blessing it could mean for God's returning war heroes to be honored and also to grieve the loss of their ministries and relationships. I know it would have been a great blessing to us.

October 23
Donny L. used drugs Monday night. I went to his house this morning.

I received word that M. and S. are sending $1200. That takes us through another month of our regular expense.

November 20
I'm now using a new journal... I want this one to be the one that holds the story of GoodSoil... to record in it the beginnings of how God answered prayers for GoodSoil's provisions. It will likely also contain the struggles and 'wildernesses' of GoodSoil's beginnings. Hope I am up to it, though; honestly, I'm a mess right now. Physically I am near the breaking point. Emotionally, I am spent, with little reserve for creativity. Spiritually I feel dry, but am fixing my ever-wandering eyes on Jesus.

I went through this during some of the early years in Africa. I have not learned how to avoid it, but I have discovered the power/secret of moving through it -- Jesus. Putting my thoughts and affections (in that order) on Him somehow pushes me up and through. That's where I am as I begin this journal. I'm looking for Jesus, struggling to discipline myself on a daily basis to look at Him in the Scriptures and talk with Him in prayer. These two simple disciplines hold so much power and blessing.

My challenge is knowing how to move from being an undisciplined person to becoming a disciplined one. Self-control is not easily developed by those who lack the very thing required to achieve it. It's like telling a non-swimmer to swim, or a kid who has never driven, "Get in and drive." I keep sinking; running off the road quickly. Yet, I recall times when God seemed to take the controls and off we went -- autopilot. I think the LORD releases help for us when we really try. The problem is that I easily get sidetracked and find myself again operating on 'me-power.'

This entry exposes my personal frailties. While I am not proud of them, I have decided to share them to illustrate that perfection is not necessary for God's work. Right direction is, however. Levites, priests, and leaders like Moses, David, and Joshua were all human and flawed. They struggled with obedience and faith and consistency. And this is exactly the point -- they struggled. They tried. They kept trying. They never gave up. They wanted to be obedient. Their hearts were rightly directed Godward even if their life actions weren't perfect. Paul said, "I strain toward the prize."

Of course, God's grace for our frailties is no license for sloth or sin. "Should we continue to sin that grace may be abundant? May God silence such a thought!" (Romans 6:1-2). God's grace is not an invitation to relax, but additional space for us to continue our pursuit of the riches found only in "Jesus, the author and PERFECTOR of our faith."

November 24
Well, bad news. Someone stole a chainsaw out of my truck. I had borrowed it, so I am responsible for replacing it. A new one costs in the range of $850-$900. That's half of our monthly income! Right now I have about $400 in the bank. I have withdrawn my IRA retirement -- which should arrive next week. I will need about $4000-$5000 of that

money for house construction materials. I must get the roof on before the worst of the winter weather arrives. I am really worn from working on the house.

"O LORD,

I have entered this ministry of faith, returned to help my mother, and taken no loans because I have believed them not to be Your will. I have trusted You, and to this point, You have been faithful. I do not expect that You'll fail me now; however, I admit to fear and trembling until You appear and act. I suppose this is part of the refining process -- to relax even before the answer, to remain calm during the storm. Care for us now, O LORD. Please provide for us and GoodSoil."

Crying to You,
Stephen

December 13
We moved into the basement of our new house today -- exactly four years from the day we arrived in Jellico! We have boxes everywhere. I am exhausted from the push to get us to this point, but at the same time exhilarated at finally being in our house.

Several weeks prior to moving into the new house, we hosted two guests who were in need of a safe place. They remained with us until the latter part of January. From the first day we lived in our new house it went into service as a place of ministry. In the fourteen years since moving into our home, God has sent more than 4000 overnight guests. The largest group to date has been sixty-one people who stayed with us for eight days! Our good neighbors and partners through many years, Steve and Claudia Greek, completed their house about the same time as we did ours and, besides their own guests, have often received the overflow from our groups. Without them we could not have served as many or as often as we have. The Greeks, their home, their friendship, and their hospitality have been another level of God's faithful provision for us.

December 28

My family and two guests have been living in the basement portion of our new house since the 13th. We moved in on Donna's birthday. I was pleased to give it to her as a gift.

God has provided so abundantly for us these four months since beginning our faith mission.   In the past three weeks He has sent the following gifts:

• One turkey (Someone in a green truck left it. We didn't know them.)
• An anonymous gift of $300. The note said, "A Friend."
• Two gifts of $200 from B. Family.
• Two gifts from Mark B. of $70 and $140.
• $50 from Brian C.
• $18 insurance refund.
• $14.39 commission from Excel Telecommunications
• One new computer
• $250 from Peggy W.
• $70 from Linda B.
• $50 from Lora A.
• $100 from Murphy C.
• Two Scriptures "from the mouth of the Lord," from Anna D.
• Prayers from David W.
• Encouragement from Jim A.
• One pizza meal from Dave V. Family
• Groceries from Kathy D.
• One free computer repair from David D.
• One day's plumbing work on the house by Mr. Carithers
• Several bunches of turnip greens from Mr. D.

December 29

The YTD total of cash supplies from my work at HTR plus donations from individuals is approximately $29,959.92.

December 31

God has finished the year with a fanfare! Today we received more assurances of His awareness and tender care for us:
- $50 from L. Adams
- $50 from the Hutchins
- $200 from Dwane P.
- I was told of a surprise gift on the way from Lori S. of an unknown amount.
- I have also been promised the return of my $300 deposit on the Florence Avenue house.

[Last days at Florence house]

[Framing the roof]

[House group effort]

[Picnic on the land]

2000 - NUDGED

January 1

I want to reflect this morning on the LORD's dealings with me over the past four years. In summary, He has been good. On the other hand, I have been weak more than strong, but always, by God's grace, able to desire the LORD and His will. This has been the gracious working of His Spirit in me, and I am deeply grateful.

We have now been 100% dependent upon the LORD for material supplies for four months. I have not calculated the exact dollar amount He has sent us, but know that we have enjoyed meats, fresh vegetables, entertainments of various kinds, clothing, and cash gifts from the hands of His servants and messengers.

People we never expected to know of our ministry or us are regularly praying for us. Our health is wonderful. Mom is so much improved in her health that she threw a party yesterday for about ten of her senior citizen friends! My children are well-behaved, respectful to Donna and me, and are developing a faith of their own. They can work hard or play hard, and they know when it is appropriate for either of those.

A couple of days ago, I received gifts of $450 and $500 from Texas and $150 from Texas George's family -- kind signs of God's awareness.

In late January, all the metal was finally installed on our roof. The workers could not begin working until 10 a.m. each day because the ice had to melt first. Watching them, the knot in my stomach was as real as the 40 feet between the ground and the peak of my roof! I prayed for the workers every day. It brought me both physical and emotional relief when all the men were at last safely on the ground again! Thank the LORD no one was injured.

[Finished metal roof]

January 16

My prayer requests today are:

- Bill W. -- healing
- Ritchie B. -- salvation
- D. and T.L. -- renewal

- Mission Camp Campers and all supplies
- Patty B.'s sister -- healing
- Tom M. -- salvation
- My son -- self-control
- Appalachia -- revival
- J.B. -- overcome resentment
- My Family -- development of their spiritual relationship with God

January 19
It is evening, and I am before the Lord, asking, "OK. Lord, what is it? What do You want?" The thought came,

"Just *you*. Just to have you here before Me."

January 21
Things are more difficult. Prayer is not as easy. My mind is less clear.

On this same day that prayer seemed so difficult, I made this entry in my journal,

Just now, while in prayer and listening I had these thoughts: "I am about to do a new thing in all the Earth. Nation will rise against nation and kingdom against kingdom, but the Word of the LORD will go forth in all the earth. I will do it, and a light shall shine in China."

I then questioned, "What is my part? What am I to do?" The answer was, "I will let you know in time."

I replied, "Yes, LORD! Send out Your Word to all the earth; shine in China. I will wait on You."

Four years passed after this entry. Jerry, a young man from Texas, visited GoodSoil as part of a spring break mission trip with a campus ministry from

Dallas. I invited him to return that following summer and serve as a GoodSoil intern. He did and was baptized in our creek during his six weeks with us. Later, in 2006, Jerry lived, served, and trained under us for eight more months in our apprenticeship. God transformed Jerry during those months, and he left us a much more sober-minded and spiritually mature young man. After his apprenticeship he returned to Texas as a sincere disciple of Christ.

A year after he left our apprenticeship, we learned that Jerry had rekindled a relationship with Julie, a young lady he knew before coming to be with us. The progress of their relationship and other news about them trickled in to us through e-mails and mutual friends. Jerry and Julie eventually married and shortly thereafter participated in a mission with the short-term missions organization Let's Start Talking. After a lot of 'back and forths,' as Jerry put it, about whether they should go to China, they decided to relocate to Beijing, learn Mandarin, and lead people to Jesus. They spent five years there making disciples (and having two children). After their mission service in China, Jerry was invited by his former campus ministry to be their campus minister. He accepted that position in 2014.

Not until writing the final portions of this book did I make the connection between my thoughts and prayer on this date in 2000 and Jerry's five years in Beijing. This private exchange between the LORD and myself would have been lost except for this entry in my journal. Yet, fifteen years later, the undeniable facts exist that God sent me a thought, that I prayed accordingly, and that Jerry went to China. I don't understand all about prayer. I don't know why I was prompted to pray for China that day. I don't know if my prayer was pivotal, or if it was one among a host of prayers God required for China. I don't have answers; I have questions, like, if I had not been praying that day, would God's plan have been spoiled or delayed? Would Jerry have been sent somewhere else? I cannot answer those questions. I don't suppose anyone can, but I can report that one day while praying, the thought came to me that God would bring a light to China; my part would be made known in time. Jerry came to us, and China was given light.

The mystery of these things is not problematic to me. It should not be offensive to you either. If prayer were mere science, it would not be prayer. The fact that God and prayer are beyond our ability to dissect, predict, or control confirms that prayer is a spiritual event. It is other. Its roots and fruits rely upon God's sovereignty and wisdom and not man's expectations or understanding.

Read Paul's prayer for those at Ephesus and ask yourself: What is it about this prayer that can be clearly understood? While Paul is hoping the saints will understand more, it is apparent that even he is stretching, searching, grasping for human vocabulary sufficient to express what he hopes the Ephesians will someday experience. If we were to compare him to a science professor with his lab students, we might envision him dissecting a frog, holding up the individual organs for examination, and explaining their inner workings in hopes his students might understand life. But life cannot be bottled; held to a microscope; or placed in the hand. It has physical characteristics, but it itself is not simply physical. Life is other.

"I keep asking that the God of our Lord Jesus Christ, the glorious Father, may give you the Spirit of wisdom and revelation, so that you may know Him better. I pray also that the eyes of your heart may be enlightened in order that you may know the hope to which He called you, the riches of his glorious inheritance in the saints, and his incomparably great power for us who believe. That power is like the working of His mighty strength which He exerted in Christ when He raised him from the dead and seated him at His right hand in the heavenly realms, far above all rule and authority, power and dominion, and every title that can be given, not only in the present age but also in the one to come. And God placed all things under His feet and appointed Him to be head over everything for the church, which is His body, the fullness of Him who fills everything in every way." -Ephesians 1:17-23

Years ago, in Kenya, I discussed the physical and unseen realities with an African spiritist. I challenged his belief that every newborn child is the return of a deceased relative. Young, eager, but ignorant, I approached the discussion as a typical western-minded thinker applying logic and science. The conversation went something like this:

I asked the spiritist, "You say this child is your deceased grandfather, and that it is so with all in the Kalenjin tribe. My question is that since there are more Kalenjin people today than ever in history, where have all the extra spirits come from?" His answer was neither a stretch of truth or logic, nor lacking in an understanding of the unseen. He shrewdly replied with a question of his own: "When you plant maize, you plant a single kernel, but when you harvest, how many kernels do you harvest?" Suddenly, my eyes were opened. He, with respect and wisdom, revealed how little I understood about spiritual mysteries. We must not approach the intangible as we do the tangible. But he was not finished. He asked, "In the Bible, there is a man who said he had many spirits in him. Also, in the Bible, all the Apostles have the Holy Spirit. Is this true?" I had to agree. He continued, "So, many spirits can live in one person, and one spirit can live in many people. So, how do you explain that?" He was right. I was ignorant. I did not understand spiritual matters. When we attempt to explain the unseen we must leave physical science and leap to something more like quantum physics -- a whole other realm.

One day, in 2015, I was walking and praying. Sometimes I pray using the pattern of the tabernacle to guide my thoughts. For example, starting with the altar, I offer thanks (thank offering) or reaffirm my complete allegiance to God (burnt offering). On this particular day, as I reached the pinnacle of a hill I climb on my prayer route, I was praying about the altar of incense. This piece of furniture is in the Holy Place and represents the prayers of the Saints. Reaching the top of the hill, I envisioned my prayers crossing, like the smoke and aroma of the incense, from the Holy Place to the residence of God -- the Most Holy Place. Prayer is a portal between realities; the point at which we may enter into the future life while still in this one. Mystery! *(More thoughts about prayer and the tabernacle in my April 1 entry)*

January 23
Last night I prayed (I'd missed praying in the morning) and asked God to help me never miss Morning Prayer again.

Consistency is a great challenge to me. It is not easy to be steady. I am a good starter but a poor finisher, and in between I'm an up-and-downer. Yet consistency is a godly trait. God is never changing, everlasting, never failing.

Creation expresses His constancy in the cycle of the seasons, the waxing and waning of the moon each month, and the cycle of day and night. I believe it is a godly trait to be consistent. It is of benefit to follow this divine pattern evident in creation. Yet I am not consistent -- it's a battle for me. Reading my journal entries, you'll find a man who is hot, then cold, then hot again, but you'll also witness a God who is faithful to constantly forgive my inconsistency. Indeed, He is my righteousness (Romans 7 and 8).

January 27
As I began praying today, the Lord caused me to realize that I should slow down, more thoughtfully approach Him, and carefully regard the greatness of His majesty. In short, I shouldn't enter His presence with so much familiarity but more respectfully and with a sober consideration of the One to whom I am speaking.

February 27
While praying today about the Appalachian church planting effort, I contemplated the need for a place where we can host meetings and invite people to hear the Word. I had the same thoughts last night also.

February 28
Today, the Lord blessed me in prayer. It was not a long prayer, but a meaningful one.

"Lord, I want Your will. I believe it is Your will for me to live by faith and give myself to the ministry of Your Word. This is my understanding. If I'm right, then do honor Yourself and glorify Your Name in this way. If not, if I am wrong or have misunderstood, then put me in Your will. Lead me to the place of Your choice. I want Your will. I want You. Amen."

This position of humility and open-handedness before God

gives me peace. I think it is the right posture.

Over ensuing years, I would return to this singular prayer. If an angel had visited me, if a hand had written it, or if the voice of God had thundered the command, "Live as Müller!" then I would have found it easier to pursue this course. But none of these were provided. I obeyed a very small, soft voice; a strong and persistent sense that following Müller's lead was God's wish for me. This unyielding conviction has been the thin, yet strong, thread tethering me to this position of prayerful dependence.

February 29
It is our prayer that through GoodSoil we may provide financial assistance to God's people. This month God used GoodSoil to donate $50 to the mission work of Helen C. in South Africa, $50 to Sara R. for her summer mission to Ukraine, $200 to the needs of Jan T. in Uganda, and $40 to assist a local family in their time of need.

March 2
Reaching home this evening, there was a letter from the Goodmans with a gift. The gift was for $5000.00! We rejoiced, knelt for prayer, and offered praise and thanksgiving! I'm numb. God, You ARE attentive to our prayers. *(See prayer request of 11/24/99)*

March 3
I'm 'infecting' myself again this morning by reading George Müller's biography. There is much to challenge me -- much! For example, he speaks on the topic of the wickedness of treating parenthood with contempt. This raises the question, 'Should we have more children?' I am 41. But Muller makes a point -- which I admit has been on my heart before -- about the godly succession through future generations.

Our son, Joshua Colton, was born 15 months later on 06/14/01.

March 11
West S. called to discuss the financial requirements for a Mission Camp. He had requested the budget particulars a few weeks earlier, which I sent him per his request. The total amount needed was $8300. On the phone tonight -- after having gone over each item in the projected budget -- he said, "We want to send you $10,000.00."

Though this news was very thrilling, the exchange of this large financial gift felt hardly any more momentous to either of us than if we'd passed a paper napkin to each other. Indeed, this amount was substantial, and GoodSoil had never received a larger single donation; yet neither West nor I credited the gift as being worthy of special merit. We both recognized that all things, whether dollar bills or paper napkins, are from God and that we are merely stewards. The conversation and ensuing transaction were the most rightfully balanced experience of gift giving and receiving I have personally ever experienced.

Comparing this entry with my 'all time low' entry on 3/8/97 there had been obvious growth in our faith and trust of Jehovah Jireh, The LORD Provides. The change, however, in no way lessened our gratitude and thankfulness. I would compare our change to that of a man rapelling over the edge of a dizzyingly high cliff for the first time. Reasonably, on his first attempt his heart rate is higher and the lump in his throat larger as he releases his full weight on to the unproven ropes, but his pulse is less stimulated on subsequent descents. At some point, his attention transfers from fear and doubt to trust and joy. The fall becomes fun as anxiety gives way to exhilaration. It was with the gift from West S. that I first recognized anxiety's waning and the emergence of a confidence that God truly would be as faithful to us as He had been to King David and King Jesus.

March 14

Wendell B., longtime missionary to Africa, told me of an African evangelist's widow who is now destitute. I had a nudge that perhaps I should send her $200 from GoodSoil. On the way home, I thought more about it and decided to definitely send her the money. Then, before I could get to my checkbook and write the check, God placed $100 in my hands from the David B. family and $200 from T.A. Both donations were to GoodSoil. God loves to fill an empty cup.

Let me attempt to provide clarity about my use of the term "nudge." It is more than a thought. I may think of something but have no sense of urgency or responsibility to act on that thought. There are times, however, when I have a thought accompanied by a strong sense of responsibility and urgency to act on it. Often, in spite of this sense of obligation, I may delay any action or even forget it altogether. Later, perhaps a few hours or weeks, the same thought will surface. Again, it will be accompanied by a sense that I am being personally called to take action. If I delay once more, it may soon return again. Now, each time I postpone action, there is guilt and added pressure that if I should fail, something of God's perfect hope for others or me may be lost.

There are a few instances in the Bible that seem to support this totally subjective event.

*Exodus 25:2 -- "Speak to the [Israelites], and let them bring to me a contribution. You will receive my contribution for every man **whose heart prompts him**." (Living English Bible)*

*2 Kings 12:4 -- "Then Jehoash said to the priests, 'All the money of the sacred things which is brought into the house of the LORD, in current money, both the money of each man's assessment and all the money which **any man's heart prompts him to bring** into the house of the LORD...'" (New American Standard Bible)*

*Job 20:3 -- "When I hear a reproof that dishonors me, then my understanding **prompts me to answer**." (New English Translation)*

*Proverbs 14:14 -- "The backslider in heart (from God and from fearing God) shall be filled with (the fruit of) his own ways, and a good man shall be satisfied with (the fruit of) his ways (with the holy thoughts and actions **which his heart prompts** and in which he delights). (Amplified Bible)*

*Romans 8:15 -- "You have not for the second time acquired the consciousness of being -- a consciousness which fills you with terror. But you have acquired a deep inward conviction of having been adopted as sons -- a conviction **which prompts us to cry aloud**, "Abba! Our Father!" (Weymouth New Testament)*

These promptings are what I'm calling a nudge. It is more than mere whim; it is 'deep inward conviction' and is included in what the New International Version of the Bible translates "being led by the Spirit of God" in Romans 8:14.

"For those who are led by the Spirit of God are the children of God."

It is a prompting agreeing with all the truths of revealed Scripture, but accompanied by an urgent and personal duty. Turning away from it produces guilt. Obedience yields peace, spiritual growth, and maturity in faith and relationship with God.

I quickly admit that this is a highly subjective topic, which means it is open to gross error. I also realize how difficult it is to provide strong theological support from the biblical text, though the passages above clearly refer to something akin to my 'nudge.' I am being honest here when I recommend exerting caution. Not every thought that appears to agree with Scripture is one that should be followed. Guilt alone is not a good barometer of God's will. As a safeguard, it is best to first take 'nudges' to wise, godly, mature Christians before taking action -- especially if the nudge might involve a dramatic action on your part. God is not pushing; He is inviting. He is not in a hurry; He is patient. He will not judge us by how quickly we discern His will, but by our willingness to act upon it.

I do not think it is wise to assume that a compelling thought is a nudge by God until it has been prayerfully and wisely vetted to determine whether it is or it is not the Spirit's prompting. I believe God extends a great deal of patience toward us as we discern these matters. However, if fully convinced that the Spirit of God is urging a specific action, I encourage humble and prompt obedience.

March 18
Tonight, I began trusting God for daily provisions AND praying for souls. This, for me, was a big and welcome step.

April 1
The ease of prayer has been absent for several days.

Prayer is difficult work; consistent prayer is even more difficult. We can understand why through the picture of prayer in the Temple. As I introduced earlier, Solomon's Temple contained several pieces of furniture. These furnishings have significance beyond their obvious functions in that they teach us about unseen realities. For example, the lampstand (menorah) is at once tangible light and symbolic of eternal light (Torah). The bread of the presence was physical bread but also representative of the coming Bread of Life -- Jesus. The third item within the Holy Place is the altar of incense. This "one cubit by one cubit" stand enlightens us concerning the magnificence and the essential nature of prayer. The burning incense is often associated with the rising prayers of Israel. Here are two examples:

Psalm 141:2 -- "May my prayer be set before you like incense; may the lifting up of my hands be like the evening sacrifice." (New Living Translation)

Revelation 8:4 -- "The smoke of the incense, mixed with the prayers of God's holy people, ascended up to God from the altar where the Angel had poured them out."

Incense is the product of pressure, crushing, and grinding; similarly, our prayers rise in seasons of trial and affliction. Reduced to our elemental finiteness, our limitedness, our neediness... our prayers ascend, "O God!" Petitioning, groaning, and penitent, humble, sincere supplication are difficult because they demand that we recognize how little we bring, how little we have, and how little we are. Yet it is here, at the point that we see how great is our departure from godlikeness, that we are finally able to connect with Deity.

The incense was then set afire by a holy flame, producing a fragrance pleasing to God. A visible smoke and an invisible aroma rose to fill the Holy Place and slipped beyond the veil into the Most Holy Place. This concoction of visible and invisible, born from pressure and fire, was daily permitted to pass into the inner chamber and into the presence of God. Not even the High Priest was privileged with such immediate and daily admission. In comparison, our requests, praise, thanksgiving, supplication, cries, and moanings are afforded both daily, immediate, and intimate access to Him.

*"I will accept **you as fragrant incense** when I bring you out from the nations and gather you from the countries where you have been scattered, and I will be proved holy through you in the sight of the nations."* –Ezekiel 20:41

*"For **we are** to God **a sweet smell of Christ**, in them that are saved, and in them that perish." -2 Corinthians 2:15*

Prayer bridges the seen and the unseen. For as God's breath left Him to enter the clay body of Adam, so the breathed prayers of the saints, in some wonderfully metaphysical way, enter the Creator's heart. Prayer is in some respects very 'human'; in some respects, it is quite 'extra-terrestrial'; in all respects it is present communion between the temporal and the eternal, between the now and what shall be. Like Noah's dove exiting his window to bring home the olive branch, prayer is the means by which we reach beyond the confines of our fleshly vessel into the heavens and touch the Life that is coming.

June 28
The Lord has put on my mind that He desires the journaling of my thoughts and a record of the experience of His workings in and through me to bring honor to His Name.

The written record of God's working in a life can have a powerful and significant effect on those who read it. I believe He wants me to write and share the events of these years.

July 5
Sunday, we baptized Kim G. in our creek.

I was invited to participate in delivering relief money to Kenya by assisting with language translation needs between the donors and the recipients. I agreed to go but did not have travel funds for myself. Though I did mention to several that I was traveling and that I would carry any of their donations toward the relief needs, I did not mention my own travel need to anyone. As with all other matters associated with trusting Him for our provisions, I had committed my personal need to secret prayer. I was therefore especially pleased when a note was enclosed with one particular gift from R.S.C. The journal entry is next:

July 7
Blessings in the mail! This morning received several gifts in answer to specific prayer requests. R.S.C. sent $2000 for famine relief. A note was enclosed stating that it was "to help with some funds for your trip and the food." This was especially powerful since I'd only mentioned to him that I was taking gifts for food, but had not mentioned that my personal travel expenses were not covered. God knows every need.

July 24
We had decided that a minimum of 20 campers was needed for our Africa Mission Camp. God sent exactly 20 campers. What a great group of kids! Surely the world will be changed through them!

From this group, several entered into cross-cultural mission work as adults.

Two joined a team and initiated a mission to Tanzania among Muslim communities. One is in Zambia working with Animists. One is making plans for Mozambique. One learned Russian and served God in Kazakhstan. One is in an undisclosed location serving God internationally in a high-risk area. Another became a minister in the US. Several entered into short-term missions in foreign locations. Others are serving in the inner city, some in business, some as teachers, as parents, or church leaders with missional hearts -- seeking to draw others to Jesus.

[Africa Mission Camp]

August 14

Phillip Hill (not his name) has been a great discouragement to me. He has expressed that he'd been disappointed in my decision to return to the US to assist my mother. He could not imagine that another avenue wasn't possible. He'd also twice expressed concern that our choice to be in Appalachia was a mistake (due to an apparent lack of receptivity there). However, I remain convinced that what we have done has been according to God's direction and will. I too am disappointed at the slow growth (two converts in five years), but we do not feel free to leave Appalachia. If we do leave, how will they ever know?

Rereading my entry on this date, it may appear that we thought ourselves the sole witness for God in Appalachia. This was not our thinking. God had been at work in Appalachia ahead of us! Before our arrival, there were people of strong faith, deep commitment, and sincere love for God and man in the mountains. Yet it is also true that in spite of the presence of these faithful ones, the culture in and around Jellico remained in need of redemption. It seemed to us that God, unwilling to give up on even the hardest heart, was attempting to work through us in providing a fresh approach to those who had resisted the efforts of those before us. We believed some would come to know God through the fresh witness of us 'foreigners.'

August 24
Tonight Michelle K. called with exciting news. Rachael has asked to be baptized Sunday! I had prayed yesterday and today that God would lead her to be united with Him in baptism! Michelle explained that as they were reading about John the Baptist, Rachael asked what baptism was and then asked to be baptized.

September 1
Praying against local evil and corruption.

September 19
I am very encouraged by Andrew Murray's writings on intercession. I am seeing how *essential* it is to keep one's mind set on heavenly things.

"Since, then, you have been raised with Christ, set your hearts on things above, where Christ is, seated at the right hand of God. Set your minds on things above, not on earthly things." -Colossians 3:1-2 (NIV)

October 4

Spoke today in several classes at Lubbock Christian University in Lubbock, Texas. After one of them, a student came up to me and said, "I think God wants me to give you all the money I have in my billfold. I have $17." That evening the cost of our meal was $17.38.

October 6

On the way back to Tennessee, we stopped to see a friend in Longview, Texas. He took me to the church's office and told the secretary to OK a tank of gasoline for us. Then he put a $50 bill in my hand. That evening we treated ourselves to Cracker Barrel. The tab came to $50 and a few cents.

November 11

D.D. and B.D. came to our weekly discussion about Jesus. Near the end of the meeting B.D. said, "I wonder if Dad would come?" I've been praying for her dad for several months.

I learned that D.D. is a gifted musician and singer. He says he will sing for us at our next meeting. I had asked God to send us "a singer" on 6/23/95.

Prayer is heard immediately, but answers are not always given or seen as quickly. B.D.'s dad did not attend that next meeting, or the next, or ever, but as of 2014, B.D.'s dad, mom, sister, and two nephews are regularly attending church and worshipping together locally on Sundays! God worked to turn her dad's heart toward righteousness over a decade after my request. A request for God to act is powerful and effective. He answers in due season. I believe this is why Jesus instructed His disciples to "pray and never give up" (Luke 18:1). God has plans that we cannot imagine. Thirteen years after this November 11th evening, a powerful ministry would be launched in this building where D.D. and B.D. met me. The exciting details will be shared in later chapters.

November 24

Helped deliver Thanksgiving meals in town. More meals than needed were donated. As a result, our family enjoyed seven wonderful hot home-cooked Thanksgiving meals! Donna felt too badly to cook for us due to the extreme nausea she experienced during pregnancy, but God provided prepared meals complete with dessert!

November 28

Ken B. called a few days ago. He is managing a land sale arrangement and believes he will receive approximately 300 acres. If it happens, he wants GoodSoil to have 15-30 acres for the camp.

There are many answers to our prayers, but more persistence in prayer is needed for ALL the answers. I must keep in mind that the main thing is not that the supplies be received through prayer, but about the witness answered prayer is to God's nearness and activity in our lives.

Three times in ten years I was told someone was considering a donation of a tract of land or resources for the Mission Camps. None has ever transpired. The clear question is, "What happened?" My answer is, "Who knows?" People can fail, and as a result, God's plan is rerouted, postponed, or thwarted. We can assume that what is or may happen is of God when it is not. These are unclear waters, and speculation can take us in all directions. For myself, I have concluded that I cannot be responsible for others' action or inaction. I can only control my part of any work for or of God. In each of the three situations regarding land or resources for our camps, I was prompt and faithful in everything I was requested or was required to do. I believe God is pleased with me, even if His larger plan may not have come about. In Ken B.'s case, he did not receive the land, but I believe his intentions will be blessed as if he had given it.

I will reiterate this principle again when the account of our second offer of property for Mission Camp is made, because I believe we need to understand this concept; we need a greater sense of how terrifically important our prompt and full obedience is in the scope of God's mighty hopes and dreams for the world and His Kingdom.

December 29

Total provisions to GoodSoil Ministries this year came to $54,161.40. Of this amount, $46,083.34 were donations while $8,078 came from Mission Camp fees. $21,500 was used for our personal income; $640 was given to charity in Appalachia; $838.53 was for evangelism in Appalachia; $6202 went to famine relief in Kenya; $10,807.78 was for the training of future missionaries through Mission Camp; $9730.12 supported other missionaries; and $3321.25 was for office equipment, supplies, study materials, registration fees, and a part-time assistant.

2001 - JOSHUA COLTON & THE INTERNS

January 1

This evening Mr. Carithers, my neighbor, asked me to do a few things at his house since he and his wife are snowbound out of state. He gave me instructions related to his needed care for house and animals and added, "The hens may have some eggs. You need to take the eggs home with you since they'll freeze tonight." We enjoyed six brown farm-fresh eggs the next morning! These were the first of God's provisions for 2001.

January 4

Had a good deal of difficulty in prayer this morning. Spent the entire hour sort of lumbering before God. The last five minutes were more encouraging. Spent four hours with D.D. (the singer) today. He took me to visit Joe and Derrick, but neither was home. We went to see Cliff B. and I shared from the Word with him.

Ten years passed after this journal entry, during which the Lord faithfully cared for GoodSoil through many ups-n-downs. At the same time, Cliff B. went through his own series of 'ups-n-downs' away from the Lord, but in 2012 he truly fell in love with God. In 2014, God worked through Cliff to found Springs of Life -- a Christ-based addiction recovery center for men. I now serve on the board of Cliff's ministry. Beyond prayers and a few discussions, I had only a minor part in Cliff's journey to Christ; I nonetheless enjoy a deep satisfaction seeing such vibrant, healthy fruit from those prayers and discussions. As sure as a farmer planting seed in the soil will one day discover a seedling, so what is done according to the will of God will not return void -- even though it may be long until fruition (1 Corinthians 15:58). I'll include more of Cliff's story in the final chapter.

January 9
Gwyneth C. called to tell me about someone who owns 12 rooms in an Italian castle. He wants to know if we can use them for Missions Camp.

Over a decade after this entry, nothing has come of this promising prospect. This, and other incidents like it, which appeared to be the hand of God but never transpired, has caused me to ponder what has actually happened. I surmise that either what I thought might be Him at work was, in fact, not; or it was His hand in action, but the individual(s) responsible did not follow through on a prompting God sent to them. People fail. They forget. They drop the ball. They rebel and reject the promptings of God. God is sovereign, but He is not a dictator; our obedience often determines how far or quickly His will develops in this world. This insight should move each of us to pay keen attention to the promptings of God, because when we fail, God's plans are affected, and we personally miss out on a special blessing God intended for us to know. Usually, that special blessing is a personal experience of Him.

January 19
Dan and Shar S. sent two checks. One was dated 1/1 and the other 1/12. The first was for $140 the second for $700! I am elated!

Last night I could not sleep. Dwane P. and I had been discussing and planning for an Eastern European Mission Camp, even though we did not have the necessary startup money. Unable to rest, I felt the strongest need to ask God for everything. So around midnight I knelt and prayed with more boldness, directness, and confidence than ever before. It was as if God Himself urged me to ask this way. I was not 'begging' God, nor was I manipulating Him; rather, my prayer this night was strictly an act of obedience. Today these two gifts from Dan and Shar came! Thank You God! Keep it up, so that others who hear of this work of Yours may be encouraged and amazed!

February 1
Immersed B.D. into Christ tonight! Her dad and mother came, along with the Greeks and my family. We borrowed Newcomb Baptist Church's baptistery. There were tears and smiles and celebration. Since she and D.D. work at nights they were wide awake afterward. I went home with them and we prayed and studied until dawn. I was exhausted, but very full. This is what I love to do!

B.D. was mentioned in the 11/8/00 entry, when she and her husband D.D. (the singer) attended a weekly discussion about Jesus.

Beginning in 2001, we hosted between two and four college interns each summer. Each group proved to be God's timely provision for us. In 2001 two summer Mission Camps were scheduled, which meant that the interns would be especially helpful, but we did not know that our son, Joshua, would be born with health complications which would demand our full attention. Only God could have known this was ahead of us. The following entries chronicle those events.

June 3
The interns (Jared and Nicole) are doing great with Africa Mission Camp. I could not carry out this summer's events without them. They are so hardworking and *talented*.

As always, God was at work ahead of us. Our son, Joshua, was born eleven days after this on the night of 6/14/01. The birth was uneventful and we took little Josh home from the hospital the same night of his birth. Our children rejoiced over their new brother, and everyone rested well. However, Joshua cried almost the whole of the second night, and at daylight on the third day his stomach had become distended and was warm to the touch. We immediately took him to the ER, where they x-rayed his abdomen. Dr. Killian calmly explained that it was an issue beyond their capabilities locally. He wanted Joshua to be taken to Children's Hospital in Knoxville, and he insisted he travel by ambulance! Donna took the ambulance with Josh. I rushed to our home to pack a few items and then meet them in Knoxville.

Upon examination in the Knoxville ER, the docs suspected cystic fibrosis. Eventually, their suspicions were confirmed. This kind of news hits like a ton of bricks. Amazing that words have such a breathtaking, blurring, dizzying effect. What do you do with a diagnosis like this? What does it mean for your child, your family, and yourself? We were unprepared -- as if anyone can be prepared for something like this. We gripped the hand of God and tried to remain optimistic and hopeful.

Some will wonder, "Where was God? Why would He allow or send such calamity on a godly family, or on an innocent child?" The true answers to these questions are found in God's character. Where was He? He was with us. Why did it happen? I don't know, but He was with us. Sin has twisted everything. Illness, failure, accidents, pain, sorrow, and trouble are but a short list of life experiences we all share -- sinners and saved alike. As I have noted earlier, suffering is part of life for us all. There are thorns for everyone. Some are asking, "What advantage is there, then, for the saved?" The saved find comfort, a place of strength, an avenue of potential aid, and the prospect of spiritual maturity in knowing that He is with them. Josh's condition was not a punishment or a failure of God's tender care and mercy. It was an opportunity for us to grow and for God to be glorified. Jesus spoke directly to this issue in John 9:1-3.

"As Jesus was passing by, He saw a man blind from birth. His disciples asked Him,

'Rabbi, who sinned, this man or his parents, that he was born blind?' Jesus answered, 'Neither this man nor his parents sinned, but this happened that the works of God might be displayed in him...'"

The physicians took our tiny, wailing, little Josh for scans, probed his tiny thin veins for blood, and conducted more exams. At times I had to leave the room -- literally on the edge of consciousness. My son's screams (and those of others down the hallways), tubes, needles, gauze, pain, etc. were overwhelming. Donna was stronger and able to manage longer stretches of the tension and turmoil. When I could stand it no more, I would withdraw to the hospital's chapel and do the one thing I could do -- petition. Facing matters beyond my ability to control, I relied upon the assurance that He was there with us and reached for my pouch of stones -- our years of answered prayers. Experience with a prayer-hearing God was my only strength. It brought me hope. Josh might be healed, but again, he might not. Either way, we knew we were not and would not be alone. We trusted God to eventually lead us through the valley of misery to a pleasant place.

Today Josh is 15. Beyond an annual bronchoscopy, he takes no regular medications for his lungs and only digestive enzymes with meals. He is lightning fast in the middle distances on his track team, as well as a pitcher and an infielder for the high school baseball team. He also plays city-league basketball and attends CrossFit every week. We filmed him at one of his workouts and used him on a YouTube video last year. Search "Meeks Spiritual Muscle" on www.youtube.com to see him in action. Beyond this, Joshua has the character of the biblical Joshua. He is tenacious, brave, and mature in his personal walk with God. He keeps the doctors scratching their heads in amazement at how well he is doing.

God graciously responded to our petitions. Donna and I could not be more blessed, but that was not yet our feeling in those early days and months of his infancy. We were overwhelmed like never before, as this next entry reveals.

June 18

The past two days and nights have been the most difficult

hours of my life. We have hardly slept at all. I have eaten nothing for two days. I existed on juice, water, and prayer-prayer-prayer. At one point today I ran out of words. I had asked for Josh's healing in every way I knew, but then, I knew of no different, new, or creative way to approach God on this issue. I was out of ammunition. Sitting before Him in silence, I recalled the story of the persistent widow. She too had tried it all, yet she did not stop. I came to the conclusion that when you've said it all, and re-said it all... then you just never give up.

God sees tenacious persistence. I am determined to persist. Jesus spoke with favor about the persistent widow, so I will keep at it myself, even if my persistence is little more than a quiet presence.

Ironically, in the midst of this grand turmoil, two of God's most memorable and meaningful provisions in my life occurred within 48 hours of arriving at the hospital with Joshua. I want to share them. I know I cannot communicate the depth of blessing they meant to both Donna and me, but I want to try.

The first came in the form of a quiet, kind, behind-the-scenes, elderly couple from our community. She was named Elizabeth. He had been a government agent and still packed a pistol. Now, they were retired and traveled the country, at their own expense, loving on very ill or dying children and their weary parents. Their ministry was one I've never heard of before or since.

By the evening of the first night in the hospital, Donna and I were beyond physically exhausted. Whatever condition is between exhaustion and death is what we had reached. The closest thing we had ever experienced to this level of fatigue was once when we traveled from Kenya without sleep for 52 hours! So, I can't recall all the details of those first days with Joshua, but I do remember that Joshua's food intake was being restricted in case of surgery. That meant that on top of everything else, hunger was gnawing at my three-day-old son. Donna could not comfort him with mother's milk. The most we could do was attempt to hold him through the tangle of wires and speak words of comfort he did not understand. I also remember the nurses had a hard time finding a vein for his IV, and that the probing at various sites in his arms and feet made him cry. It was a kind of crying that erupted in bursts and caused his body to quake violently. He was miserable, and we could do little about it. My nerves were raw. Donna was still recovering from the exhaustion of a pregnancy and delivery. We were barely holding ourselves together when there was an unexpected gentle knock on the door of our room. It was Elizabeth and her husband. The atmosphere lifted as they walked in. She went directly to Josh and lifted Josh, spasmodic crying, sock cap, wires and tubes, and all, into her arms. Her speaking calmed him a bit. "You guys rest. I've got him," she said. Donna instantly collapsed in the hospital bed; I followed suit in a chair near her.

Throughout the evening and night, Joshua cried himself to sleep for brief periods only to jolt awake again and repeat the process. Intermittently, I bolted to consciousness, checked whether all was well, and collapsed again. Always, Elizabeth was there, holding him, rocking him, walking with him, and singing over him until the sun's rays delivered a new day and renewed energy. Much of those early hours remains a blur, but I will not forget Elizabeth's singing.

A bit recharged, I renewed my vigil of prayer. Otherwise, running errands for Donna, waiting on reports and lab tests, taking calls, and updating family kept me occupied. Then, in the midst of the activity, I experienced something very rare for me -- I felt alone. I NEEDED a friend -- a man to stand with me. My only sibling lived several states away, my good friend and neighbor Stephen Greek was out of the country, and my dad had passed away when I was a teen. One person's name came to mind. When I called, he immediately arranged to come to the hospital. Six hours later, Glen Robb and I were visiting in the hospital cafeteria together over cups of coffee. Glen had been a friend since graduate studies and was now living in Atlanta. He and his wife, Nancy, were people Donna and I had admired for many years. Glen was a genuine man, a stable man, a man of faith, a man like Nathaniel -- guileless. I could trust Glen. He truly cared. He was also wise. He knew how to manage a crisis and could keep perspective under pressure. I needed all of that. I also just needed a friend, and he delivered on every count. I will never forget the ministry of presence he delivered to us on that occasion. Through Glen, God provided what I needed to hold things together and move back into a position of control and stability. May God bless him richly.

The Pediatric Pulmonologist and the medical staff at Children's Hospital in Knoxville were amazing! They handled everything so well... including Donna's and my emotions and concerns. God provided even in this. He was with us -- near and active. In the years to come God would astonish us, and the doctors, with Josh's health, though for those first two weeks we lived on pins and needles as Josh's weight continued to drop. Meanwhile, our second Mission Camp was scheduled to begin in a few days. Somehow, in the midst of everything, we managed to get Donna and Joshua home in time to kick off the Eastern European Mission Camp. I don't know how we did it, but I give the greatest credit to the capable help of the two summer interns and the work of my old employer Dwane P., who developed the Eastern European version of Mission Camp. Without them the camp could not have been held. Again, God was providing the needs of GoodSoil's ministry.

June 24

Eastern European Mission Camp has 11 campers. Dwane P. has done a great job of pulling this one off. The kids are very mature and serious. Gwyneth Curtis has been a godsend. One camper is specifically interested in Russia.

June 26

God has moved several of our campers very deeply tonight. It is delightful to see Christ being formed.

July 4

Joshua lost another ounce last week. Then Monday he had gained 2 ounces and has grown ¾ inch!!!! When I heard the news I blew God kisses, waved my hands in honor and acknowledgment of Him as the source of this blessing, and then I literally fell on my face to praise and thank Him.

I have never been so grateful for anything as I was Monday for that good news.

July 5
God has blessed and provided for our personal and ministry needs in diverse and unexpected ways: The R. family handed Donna a $2000 check toward the purchase of land for a mission camp -- if we should find a suitable location. Mr. P. also sent $1000 for mission camp land. B.M. handed me a packet of steaks a few nights ago. Stan S. sent Donna a lot of new clothes. Stan's family sent $50 for our personal expenses while Joshua was at the hospital. Mr. Carithers cut my hay for me yesterday.

While blessings poured in, we also experienced the tension of trusting God when dark clouds arise. The prospects of Joshua's cystic fibrosis and associated expenses loom large. As well, Mark B., Bruce W., and Dan S. have told me that their personal gifts will likely stop in August or September due to personal income changes. These represent about 40% of our 'regularly-expected' monthly base. (The base is roughly 40%-60% of usual monthly expenses. The balance is always God's surprise for us.) This will be a season in which our eyes will be upon the Lord afresh.

July 9
I do not think God will build His church in Appalachia through a powerful speaker but through the lives of His people. They will be the powerful 'preaching' which we will employ to save many and build a community of people devoted to the will and ways of Jesus.

July 15
Matters such as the illness of a child are heavy and never leave those involved. Though I'm busy with other life concerns, the knowledge of Joshua's situation lingers very

near the surface of every moment. Whenever there is a pause in the activity around me, concern for Josh surfaces and I am dealing with it again. I wish there were some sort of real rest or a break from it, but there is none. It's exhausting.

In every situation I've encountered in my life there was a light at the end of the tunnel. Sometimes the light did not appear for a while, but I knew one would eventually appear. This is different. I'm not in a tunnel this time; I'm in a cave. There is no exit, just a wall. I feel 'stuck' in a cave that will be my home from now on, but I am not alone in the cave. God is here. His angels are here. I am not alone, and that makes it bearable; perhaps it may one day even become preferred.

Re reading this entry 13 years later I remember that dark, alone, stuck, imprisoned feeling. Today, however, it is just a memory. As I'm writing this line, Josh is running through the house in a game of chase with his four-year-old niece as both laugh hysterically. This morning when I woke him for school, I could not help but notice his muscular arms and chest. This year he teamed with a friend and they placed second in a special CrossFit event for cystic fibrosis awareness in Knoxville. He was the only participant who actually had CF. The docs monitor him, and he goes in once a year for a pic-line antibiotic treatment. Otherwise, he takes oral enzymes with his meals, but no other regular medications! So, there are some things in our lives that are different than if he were CF free, but these have become our normal -- and it is okay. The cave isn't as awful a place as we'd imagined, and by the provision of God's grace, neither is it as awful as it could have been.

July 19
Received a pickup truck full of food as well as a freezer full of frozen foods when the World Servants group double-ordered by accident. B.M. gave us three-dozen ears of fresh corn, and today I sold our old Suburban for $1600. Wow.

July 20

The evening was filled with prayer. Spent 6 p.m. — 10 p.m. with five others from the community praying for the area. Praise the Lord for moving others to join us in prayer for the area.

July 23

Joshua gained 3.2 ounces!

August 3

Africa Mission Camp has gone *so* well. I'm hearing the campers talking about forming teams! My own son, Daniel, is thinking about Mozambique. The kids' faith is stronger and personal conviction is firming up as well. Everyone is interested in an Africa trip next summer to see and learn first-hand. I believe we will produce leaders for future mission teams from this group. I'm thrilled and relieved to know that our difficult labor has not been in vain.

Over the years, many of our MC grads went on to form or join mission teams. Several from this particular summer's camp went on to live and work in Africa. I took five on a Mission Camp trip to Kenya and Uganda a few years later.

September 1

Received three boxes in the mail from a church in Cleveland, OH. Two were full of Pampers for Joshua. The other contained fun foods like chocolates, pretzels, lemonade, etc.

September 11

Was convicted today that I must become more disciplined in the important matters: primarily prayer and ministry of the Word.

September 17

America is at war. My heart today is for the victims, but

also for the Muslims. I know that they will someday be
receptive -- at least in pockets -- and I wish we could
prepare kids who would go there after this war is over to
begin taking them The Light.

September 18
At the Lafollette Bible study we had six besides the
Daniel N. family.

This Bible study would continue weekly for three years. Daniel N. and his
wife were a childless young couple when I met them, but today they have five
children. Today they are faithful Believers and among our dearest friends.
Their children are growing in the knowledge and love of Christ.

October 2
We prayed for D. and his wife last night and drove over to
see them, but they were gone. This morning D. drove to our
house at 5 a.m. to talk. I was awake, but getting ready to
drive to Lafollette. Steve G. and I took him to breakfast
and talked. D. told us he had taken seven or eight Valiums
just before he came to see us. I think he was using us as
a place to hide from his family until it wore off. Drugs
are so powerful and controlling.

"D." is mentioned in many of my journal entries over the years. Up to now,
15 years later, he continues to occasionally feign some interest in God. Every
two or three years he will contact me with words of gratitude for what an
important person I am to him, seek my prayers and advice, and, within a day
or so, disappear into his dark and purposeless routine of chasing pills and
avoiding commitment to God and responsibility for his life. This pattern has
become an ever-deepening rut that's now a very large trench.

November 11
Returned from Searcy, Arkansas -- after a Mission Camp
recruiting trip that included travel to Oklahoma and Texas

-- around midnight. This morning I checked the accounts and only $800 were available for our October salary. It was clear that things were going to be difficult. I checked the mail on my desk. There was a bill of $117 and a gift of $150! I felt we were either on the verge of a big testimonial event or on the slippery slope of the final plunge.

On the way to buy milk for breakfast, I stopped at our mailbox. There were three letters inside. The first two contained gifts of $25 and $50. The third letter contained a check plus a note. I opened it and held my breath. It was from a group who had come last summer. They had had extra money after their mission trip and said they wanted to send us the balance. I slowly flipped over the check... $1500! I shouted! I clapped! I chanted, "He did it! He did it! He did it!"

November 14
Gene and Valerie were supposed to come to our meeting last night. They did not. Valerie had called ahead, however, to say that they might not be coming due to illness. I'm delighted because it shows me that God is working on their hearts in answer to prayer.

December 6
Yesterday God supplied us with ten boxes of cereal from a semi truck that had wrecked on the interstate. Robert R. brought it by to us. Mrs. M.C. sent $50. I'm grateful for how God has nudged her for the past couple of years to participate with us.

December 9
The day before yesterday I got a call to help M.S. take a mattress to someone in Jellico. I was very busy and did not really have time, but went anyway. When unloading the

mattress, the person to whom we were taking the mattress came out. It was T., the live-in girlfriend of R.J., whom we'd been praying for during the past two weeks! I had only been given their names but had not known where they lived, until this 'chance' meeting. God hears and acts when we pray for souls.

December 14
Praying for souls. Especially today I prayed for D. and B.B., R.J. and T., D. and G., and D.T. Received $50 in mail yesterday from Bernice W. Delighted she is in prayer for Jeannie T. and Shara S.

The GoodSoil money is depleted. We have $8000, but it has been designated for mission camp land, so I cannot use it for daily needs. Ironically, I'm sending out a booklet that details the gifts and provisions of God over the first six years, yet at present, we don't have the $300 it will cost to print and mail copies of it. I'm in prayer for that -- our eyes are on Him. He never fails and His children do not go begging for bread.

I think we are about to be tested. Afterward, if we pass the test, God will know the character of our hearts and sincerity of our devotion. I'm confident that He will send a "ram into the bushes" and we will go home rejoicing with yet another testimony with which to build faith.

December 17
In our mailbox today was a letter from Rick W. I knew it was good news since he and his wife have often been God's instruments of blessing in past years. The envelope contained a letter and a check. The letter, especially Rick W.'s last paragraph, moved me. He was so humble, saying, "Don't think we are generous. We've only been blessed..." The letter indicated he was sending not one,

but two checks. I then looked at them. They were for $500 and for $2000!

Later the same day a gift from W.S. came for $250! These provisions were plenty for our own needs and for the booklet.

The 'booklet' mentioned in this entry was actually the printing of a first version of the material in this book. *(See 12/14/01)*

December 29
This was a special day. The Lord sent a special gift through the Goodman family that was totally unexpected. They have never sent us a gift in December before, so the $5000 that arrived today came as a wonderful surprise. At other times their gifts have come when we were near the end of our resources, but this time we already had enough for the month. So we consider this gift to be an advance on next year's needs. This is such a tender gesture by the Father -- to end the year with provisions already in hand for next year.

D.D. and B.D. came by today. He is looking for a Christian rehab center. He asked me to help him find one. Praise the Lord, I thought we'd lost them.

December 31
Received a gift of $200 from P.F., but I don't know P.F.! Perhaps we have met, but I don't recall his name. His gift, though much appreciated, did not represent a tenth of the value to me that his attached note did. It said,

"The Lord put it on my heart yesterday to send this. I have no idea why, but I'm sure you and The Father know. I delight myself in Him and His will! It is my prayer that this helps fulfill some need you asked His help with. May

the Lord God grant us grace and faith to trust Him more
and more."

What more perfect way to complete my entries for this
past year of trusting God fully for our provisions than
with a note assuring me that God is listening, that He is
moving hearts, and that those hearts, even those who are
strangers to us, are responding to His nudges?

2004 - A VERY SPECIFIC REQUEST

Let us now fast-forward to 2004. After several years of growing in our faith and seeing Him supply over and over again, we had concluded 2003 on a high note. However, 2004 was to be uniquely challenging, and consequently, rewarding.

January 1

The Lord delivered to GoodSoil about $15,000.00 in the final three weeks of 2003. On December 30th I was able to write a salary check to us from GoodSoil of $10,400.00, which brought our year's total to $32,000.00! This large last salary installment enabled us to send the "P. Family" a gift of $1,300.00 to support their mission in Germany.

GoodSoil was also given $249.00 for use in local benevolence, so when Daniel N. needed his truck repaired, I was able to assist him with $100.00. *(Keep this entry in mind when reading a reference to Daniel N. in June's entry later this same year)*

Our goal for 2003 had been to give away 12% of our income, and we did it. By God's help we will be able to give more in 2004.

I don't know how we have managed this year, with the small amount we were paid until now, but God's large year-end lump-sum payment has left us with more surplus than we have ever had in our lives. We now have almost $10,000.00 to invest or save as we see best!

Shortly after the entry above I invited eight college students to come for the summer as GoodSoil interns. A part of our ministry involved training the next generation of His people and planting in their hearts an interest and desire for His mission. Usually, interns raise money for their keep. For some reason, however, this year I felt I should handle it differently; perhaps it was because we were in command of such a large surplus at the time. I told the interns, "Raise money for your personal needs, school fees, or whatever, but we will take care of all your other needs while you are here. No need to worry, God will supply for us all." I remember hearing myself say that and inwardly thinking that I might have made a mistake in telling them not to raise any funds to assist with the cost of their stay with us.

My journal is blank from the entry above until the following entry near the end of April. The two sit in ironic juxtaposition in my journal.

April 30
Financially, we are almost the lowest ever. I have approximately $450.00 in the GoodSoil account. I have a credit card bill that is larger than that amount. We have taken no salary for April. There is nothing to take. GoodSoil actually owes me about $450.00 for reimbursements. Our personal account is at about $1,700.00, but at least $1,000.00 of that has been spent for living expenses on the credit card. So we personally have $700.00 for May. That does not allow for our health insurance premium due early next month off $650.00. I'm working on what I can sell or return. I returned $450.00 of items today.

God is my main resource. I've asked Him to touch someone

to send a large gift.

May 10

Seems I make journal entries at the lowest or highest moments of our experience. Today is a low. Looks like we have $4.00 in the GoodSoil account. There are $350.00 worth of donations ready to be deposited, but $310.00 of that is for bills that are due. We took no salary in April. Our personal account is less than our bills. They won't come due for a few days, but honestly, I don't know how we'll make it this time -- except by God's intervention. I'm making a few calls today to try to further delay some of the bill paying. Also listing for sale some of our possessions on the radio swap-shop and in the newspaper classifieds.

I have been told that World Servants is sending a donation to GoodSoil soon. I don't know how much, but perhaps it will help. Anyway, it is a 'water from the rock' moment.

Yesterday, I received Jewel P.'s little envelope with $20.00 inside. (Jewel P. is a local widow who sent gifts in little envelopes when she could.) She doesn't realize how important her 'mite' is at this time. May God reward her.

Opened a Bible near my desk. I opened and read an encouraging quote I'd scribbled in it by J. W. McGarvey on Romans 8:28. "Our purpose is of such import, such magnitude, such eternal fixedness and perennial viability as to be a guarantee that God will permit no temporal accidentals to thwart it." This gives encouragement because it reminds me that I am not working off mere well-wishing, but out of truth, the facts of God and His unchanging character.

May 11

GoodSoil has about $4.00, and we personally have less than $50.00.

I keep reminding myself that the lowest point in a ministry such as ours holds the ripest potential to be its greatest moment. Yet I admit there is a sense of despair that wants to take root. Some part of me suggests, "It is over," but another, stronger part says, "No. It is not over; only farther along."

It is difficult for me to give up. I'm not one to let go without a fight, and I'll fight with whatever I have. Perhaps it is this personal tenacity that now keeps my heart afloat; perhaps it is faith in His faithfulness. I cannot honestly differentiate right now. I only know I am trying still, against the visible evidence, to hope in the unseen reality that God is, that He is good, and that He knows my heart. I have chosen instead of thinking more about our financial situation to spend most of today planning and dreaming again for the Appalachian Church and for GoodSoil Ministries.

The effort to remember that valleys are necessary for the creation of heights, to focus on Him rather than circumstances, and to push back on doubt took all I had sometimes. Twelve years after this occasion, I recorded the following journal entry:

"Facing an $11,345.00 shortfall for full funding this year, if it is not supplied in the next thirty-three days. Even after all these years of trusting and witnessing God supply us, the prospect of so much being supplied 'from nowhere' still, at first glance, seems too far-fetched. This view (looking at the problem) is always daunting, but it is so only because it is the wrong way to look at a problem. The better way, the healthy way, the Biblical way, the sane way is to view the solution -- to view God's great ability, loving kindness, and sovereignty. Both, taken together, is the correct view of any circumstance.

For example, I would certainly have reason to be concerned if I were facing a raging lion charging toward me, but no cause for alarm if I also considered the iron cage housing that lion and separating it from me. This is how we find peace and strength in even the most perilous circumstances." *(11/29/16)*

May 13
*Psalm 9:10 "Those who know your name will trust in you, for you, LORD, have **never** forsaken those who seek you."*

Psalm 91:14-16 "'Because he loves me,' says the LORD, 'I will rescue him; I will protect him, for he acknowledges my name. He will call upon me, and I will answer him; I will be with him in trouble, I will deliver him and honor him. With long life I will satisfy him and show him my salvation.'"

• God has led us to this place, to this work, and to the conclusion that prayer for provisions is required of us.
• He who commands us not to muzzle the ox will not Himself muzzle His worker. He who began a good work will not begin the construction of it and then fail to supply all that is needed.
• He who is able to supply all good gifts from heaven will not withhold them for evil intent.
• God doesn't abandon.
• He does not betray or trick.
• He fulfills everything in every way -- especially for the Church.
• He who has such compassion for the lowest elements of His ordered creation will not forget His chief element.

• He will not permit His word to fail or His Name to be dishonored, nor will He give scoffers or unbelievers a single argument for their case against Him.

• God has delivered His people -- always; water from rocks, manna and meat in the deserts, ravens in ravines, widows with jars, lepers with good news, fish and bread by the baskets, and our needs met for over a decade.

• He is a supplier who not only can supply, but also is moved by His own nature and compassions to supply.

How? How possibly could He act in any other way but to deliver and supply at the right time and in the right way? It seems it would actually be more difficult, more contrary to nature and life, for God to not supply than to supply. In fact, it would be very costly to Him, to His reputation, and to the work of Christ if He were to fail.

So we should not worry, but wait; and the waiting should only be for the provisions themselves. Meanwhile, we should continue to be busy with His work and perhaps even increase our efforts. It's a time for considering enlargement of our vision, not a time to scale back.

Often in the Psalms, when there is an expression of despair, disappointment, or dread, the psalmist will do as I have done here. He will state his concern and what is true about God's character. This pattern is seen in Psalm 10:1, 14, 17:

"Why, O LORD, do you stand far off? Why do you hide yourself in times of trouble?"

"But you, O God, do see trouble and grief; you consider it to take it in hand."

"You hear, O LORD, the desire of the afflicted; you encourage them, and you listen to their cry, defending the fatherless and the oppressed,"

Often the psalmist will include an additional item. He will recall the acts of God in the past as in Psalm 13:1, 5, 6.

"How long, O LORD? Will you forget me forever?... But I trust in your unfailing love; my heart rejoices in your salvation. I will sing to the LORD, for he has been good to me."

Some Psalms, like Psalm 107, are almost entirely a recounting of God's activity and faithfulness in times past and conclude with the admonition:

"Whoever is wise, let him heed these things and consider the great love of the LORD."

I have found it a wise practice to follow this pattern as well so that I think rightly and hopefully when I feel otherwise. Negative current circumstances are not always evidence of God's absence or unconcern. Positive current circumstances are not always evidence of God's presence or pleasure. God is simply God. We must understand and rely on that truth. When things are dark or broken, we rely on Him in the same way; but standing strong at those times can be very challenging because it is difficult to discount what is tangible. What do we do with unanswered prayer?

When the disease won, the request was not supplied, or we did not get what we expected, those facts could not be ignored. Since we began our journey, we have occasionally become aware of others who determined to trust God for supplies in the same manner as us. Some who trusted did not receive their expected help from the LORD. So, how can their experiences and ours be reconciled?

This is a fair and reasonable question that demands to be addressed. Therefore -- admitting that I do not have revelation in these matters beyond the Scriptures and my own experiences -- I will share my current view of this dilemma. First, I believe that God is sovereign. I would not describe Him as a puppet-master managing every decision or action of every person; but I do believe He is engaged in each individual's life in such a way as to give them opportunities to choose and act so they might be best benefitted. I'll illustrate through Abraham and Sarah.

Abraham had children through the natural way and order of things. He had many children, but not through Sarah. Through Hagar, and through a number of other women, Abraham had children born to him in his youth (Genesis 25:6). Why was this not so through Sarah? Was there a medical issue? Did Sarah have hidden sin in her life? Was God mad at them? What was the deal with Sarah and Abraham?

Of course, by God's goodness, we know the answer. *"Now Sarai was childless because she was not able to conceive" (Genesis 11:30).* On the surface, it appears she had a physical limitation, BUT we know this clearly wasn't the case, because she was physically able to eventually conceive and bear a child. The issue is not fertility. The delay in conception is the matter to consider. Why did God delay her conception?

Again, by God's goodness, we know the answer. We know that a son born to them far beyond their years of conception was necessary to God's building a nation of faith. In one way, it is as if they were impregnated with the seed of faith when they left Ur, nurtured the pregnancy between Haran and Abimelech, began contractions at Isaac's birth, and delivered on Mount Moriah.

The truth is God always positions us for our ultimate best. This is the most loving thing anyone could do for another. In His caring wisdom and foresight, like a mother insisting on an active toddler's nap or a coach demanding calisthenics, God wants for us what we sometimes don't know to want for ourselves. When He loves us like this, it can be as confusing and challenging as the need for a nap is to a toddler or push-ups and laps are to a guy who just wants to slip on his uniform and go to the game. Those who have a mature trust stand firm; the immature cry or quit.

"Not that I have already obtained all this… but I press on… All of us who are mature should take such a view of things… Therefore my brothers… this is how you should stand firm in the Lord." -Philippians 3:12-4:1

He works all things for the good of those who love Him and keep His commands -- meaning that for anyone who will love Him and keep His commands can do so out of trust that His choices and timing are ultimately in his/her best interest. This confident trusting of His character as a good father who sees and is looking out for our best is what Abraham first exemplified, and it is what I have come to practice on my journey of trusting God for our provisions. Neither Abraham nor I have done it without fault, but we have managed to not cry out at Him or quit. I believe that this same loving God was employing this same maturing and loving process in the lives of those we've known who trusted Him for their provisions, but who did not receive them. What I am proposing is that God's provision of money or supplies was never His MAJOR concern for us, for George Müller, or for anyone who has called out to God for help. His primary concern was to provide that which would help us answer the seminal question, "Do we trust His goodness and His nearness?"

If, in this process, we reject Him when He doesn't give us what we want or behave as we had imagined, the purpose of His withholding from us our desires is proven to be better for us than the provision of our prayer request. It illustrates that our attachment to His 'benefits' is stronger than it is His person. Showing this to us is actually a rescue from a great danger that we did not realize we faced. His choice of revealing the trip-wire in our hearts was a supreme and loving act of kindness. Indeed, the physical provision of an answer to a request might not reveal anything about our faith, whereas a request withheld is almost always a means of proving the strength or weakness, the presence or absence of our faith in God. Abraham was not commended for having Isaac. He was commended for being willing NOT to have Isaac. Whatever belief and trust in God that was required to wait upon God to bring life from a withered, lifeless womb was no faith in comparison to what happened on Mt. Moriah! Because he trusted in God in the face of *losing* what he had thought would be God's provision, our father, Abraham, was commended. There, in that instance, son bound and knife in hand, he introduces all who would follow God to the use of the new Name Jehovah Jireh -- God the Provider. It was when Abram trusted God's trustworthiness in spite of appearances that he became the father of all who would believe.

Paul holds up this kind of trust as the seed from which we, who believe in Jehovah Jireh, are born.

*"It is **not the children of the flesh** who are God's children, but it is the children of the promise who are regarded as offspring." -Romans 9:8*

*"Consider Abraham: He **believed** God, and it was credited to him as righteousness." -Galatians 3:6*

The promises were spoken to Abraham and **his seed**. The Scripture does not say, "and to seeds," meaning many people, but *"and to your seed,"* meaning one person, who is **Christ**.

In step with Paul's teaching on faith, the Faith Hall of Fame in Hebrews 11 begins, *"Now faith is being sure of what **we hope for**, and certain of what **we do not see.**"* It then concludes with a statement echoing the essence of this Abrahamic faith to the generations that will follow: *"These were all commended for their faith, yet **none of them received** what had been promised." -Hebrews 11:39*

Faith is the conviction that God is present -- even when not seen. It is relying on His loving kindness when circumstances are neither loving nor kind. The Abrahamic-faith life is lived based on the confidence that God is involved and working for our best even when sight seems to prove otherwise. Paul argues this point to the Roman community, who apparently were in a situation something like that of our friends. They weren't seeing God act in their lives as they assumed a living and loving God might. Paul's response is, *"He (God) says to Moses, 'I will have mercy on whom I will have mercy, and I will have compassion on whom I have compassion.' It does not depend on man's desire or effort, but on God's mercy" (Romans 9:15-16).* At first blush, this sounds hard. God looks like a bully. Yet, in fact, this is telling us about His perfect kindness and selfless love toward us! Evil is bad. Evil destroys. Evil hurts. Therefore, the holy and loving God withdraws from all that is evil. He hates it and will not allow evil to prosper out of control any more than a good mother might permit her child's fever to escalate to the point of danger.

Because God will not allow evil unlimited control, we are assured that those bound and determined to pursue evil (think Pharaoh) will not permanently reign unrestrained. Moreover, because God is powerful, good, and capable, the destruction of evil will be turned into eventual good for those who pursue God. As an example, Pharaoh's destruction became a standing deterrent to those who might think of following evil, while Israel's rescue offered an alluring incentive for those who might follow YHVH.

Playing the Devil's advocate, let me now ask, "Okay then, even if it is reasonable for God to withdraw from evil, how is it reasonable that He might not respond to the prayers of the faithful? Even a fairly good earthly father comes running when his child screams!"

And here are my answers:

Q. Why would our Heavenly Father not respond by supplying my friend's faithful prayers and obedience?

A. There are two possibilities. First, because, knowing all and loving perfectly, God knew those supplies were not in my friend's best interest. Second, because people fail, those God nudged did not obey, which would have prolonged his struggle until God provided for them in a different way.

Q. Is this an indication that God might not exist, or at the very least that He does not care?

A. Quite the contrary! It proves He is loving and wise.

Q. Did my friends do something to deserve punishment like Pharaoh?

A. This is not the proper comparison. They were not a Pharaoh; they were more like Moses and Israel. Unanswered prayer is not always a sign of God's displeasure. He punished evil, true; but He disciplines those He loves. Trouble is no more certain a sign of His wrath than good is evidence of His delight. Both the just and the unjust receive rain and storm. Life happens.

More regularly, the natural consequences of our and others' actions are what we witness and experience in life. Only occasionally does God intervene.

The church in Rome, I believe, was asking the question above when they complained, *"Then why does God still blame us? For who resists his will?"* -*Romans 9:19*

Shockingly, Paul's reply is not very sympathetic. He shoots back, *"But who are you, O man, to talk back to God? Shall what is formed say to him who formed it, 'Why did you make me like this?' Does not the potter have the right to make out of the same lump of clay some pottery for noble purposes and some for common use?'"*

What comes clear from Paul's answer is that God is the boss; you and I are not. "Them's the facts, ma'am." However, this is not the total picture. Paul goes on, and what he adds is inspiring!

"What if God, choosing to show his wrath and make his power known, bore with great patience the objects of his wrath -- prepared for destruction?" In other words, He lets the bad guys have it easy… meaning He lets the good guys struggle and be burdened like Israel did under Pharaoh for 400 years!

Why would God allow His people, like my friends or Israel, to suffer? Why would He force them to wait? Why might He not respond quickly when called upon? Paul answers this question with a question: "What if He did this **to make the riches of His glory known to the objects of His mercy**, whom He prepared in advance for glory – even us…" In other words, what if He did not answer their requests **because He had something *even more wonderful* in store for them?**

This opens a whole new world. The old way of thinking is, "If I do xyz, then God should respond to my actions." This is the age-old 'stumbling stone' of a works approach to God and life. A works approach is not based in relationship but rather in performance. It is contractual rather than covenantal and behaves more mechanically than mystically. At its base it is manipulative rather than trusting or unconditionally loving.

Faith, on the other hand, is all about confidence in His character; staying the course; being true to the covenant no matter the outcome; trusting in the sincerity of a loving person more than on signed lease particulars. It is an unflinching trust in the sovereignty and goodness of God when He does not appear to act. Jesus personified this faith by trusting God to His death; by believing in His goodness and ability to raise His body from the dead.

Two young boys are with their mother. One requests a piece of candy. Mom obliges and hands over a candy sucker, to the delight of the child! The younger brother sees and asks for the same. The mother says, "No, son. You can't have any."

Is this unfair? Does Mom prefer one to the other? Does she love one and not both? Has the second son done something to offend his mother? How could a loving parent be so egregiously insensitive?

On its face, this is unfair, if not callous or flatly mean. However, if there is more to the picture, a different conclusion would be drawn about the mother. What if the younger son is diabetic? What if this loving mother has learned that sugar is harmful to her youngest? What if the older son is hypoglycemic and a quick sugar rush is needed to keep his blood sugar up? What does this do to our view of Mom?

Unanswered prayer, like our friends experienced, must be weighed in light of a full picture. It is not appropriate to conclude that they were less spiritual than us, or that we are more connected with God, because He has answered our prayers for provisions. There are things involved, unseen things, that we cannot understand, but that He does. We must simply follow His ways and trust His goodness to withhold or provide as is ultimately and summarily best.

One of the young couples I have watched walk through this process did not have even their most basic needs supplied through prayer and faithfulness. They literally went dumpster diving! Would God do that to His children? Yes, IF that was the needed force to lead them to where He wanted them to be. This family, as a result of being led by God to the 'end of their financial rope,' had, of necessity, to consider alternative work vehicles. Today, they are YouTube sensations and making a very fine income while also working together as a family providing a beautiful role model to an audience that now exceeds 100,000! That would never have been theirs had God provided for them as they had initially requested.

Was their journey easy? Ha! Was it what they wanted? Of course not. Was it challenging to their faith? Certainly. Did God leave them? On the contrary, it appears that He blessed them. How should we compare their experience with ours? Is God faithfully loving both of us?

King David went through this 3,000 years before my friends. Psalm 35:13-14 says,

"When my prayers returned to me unanswered, I went about mourning as though for my friend or brother. I bowed my head in grief as though weeping for my mother."

Even David wrestled with God's silence, but he held the line. He stayed with God. He looked ahead and declared in verse 28,

"My tongue will speak of your righteousness and of your praises all day long"

Of course, we all know the end of his story; he did well to trust God's faithfulness through those times of quiet, lonely suffering. Like that good mother, God does what is best rather than what we feel is best (think Job.). He does for us what is ULTIMATELY most beneficial. In the meantime, the effort we invest to trust Him through the 'no candy for you' is neither missed nor dismissed by God. Though we may question, wrestle, groan, and complain during the process, our tenacity is what God seeks. The "Heroes of Faith" in the Hebrews 11 list are some who practiced this.

I encourage you to take a slow walk through this Hebrews 11 Hall of Fame because I'm betting you've missed something critical in past readings of it. Listen, with fresh ears, to what is said about that group.

*"They were stoned; they were sawed in two; they were put to death by the sword. They went about in sheepskins and goatskins, destitute, persecuted and mistreated -- the world was not worthy of them. They wandered in deserts and mountains, and in caves and holes in the ground. These were all commended for their faith, yet **none of them received what had been promised**."* -Hebrews 11:37-39

The chapter begins with commendation of those whose faith held steady despite lack of any tangible results. Abel was commended as a righteous man and one who pleased God. Abel, along with all these others, and along with our friends, are a unique 'club' -- they are martyrs. They died doing the right thing. Some died physically, others financially, and some paid a high emotional price following Him to their last dollar or their last ounce of sanity. The Greek word here is 'martyreo,' from which comes the English word martyr. It means "witness." Ironic, isn't it? A witness tells what they have seen; yet none of these saw what they hoped for. Clearly, martyrs are a special category of witnesses who give testimony to unseen reality. Think about that.

Prayer is about relationship, not requisition. It is entering the office of the King of Heaven to submit my thoughts at the feet of His decisions. Here, in the safe and welcoming company of my Father, I am given audience. I can be myself without fear of wrath or judgment. It is a place where God and I work together for the good, and where I then wait on His wise and loving decisions. Prayer and faith primarily provide a platform for communion with Him who loves me most and best.

Prayer answers delight us; delays arouse despair. We present our needs. God does what is best. The mature accept and embrace this standard for their lives, understanding that God will reward them for praying whether He gives them what they ask for or not.

*"But when you pray, go into your room, close the door and pray to your Father, who is unseen. Then your Father, who sees what is done in secret, will **reward** (not necessarily answer) you."* -Matthew 6:6

I know I haven't addressed every quandary on prayer. I don't have all the answers. I'm on the journey too. But if what I've offered doesn't seem sound, then this is my advice: *"Always pray and never give up"* (Luke 18:1). Jesus said it this way, *"Be ever knocking, ever seeking, always asking… He will answer"* (Matthew 7:7-8 my paraphrase).

May 14
Matt R. gave $249.00 to GoodSoil!

May 17
Sold an old garden tiller yesterday for $150.00. I've had several calls on the tractor we put up for sale, but no takers. We personally received $25.00 from Brad S. GoodSoil received $250.00 from West S. and $200.00 from the Antioch Church.

May 18
Spoke to a small gathering at the Jellico Community Hospital. They gave me a $25.00 gift certificate. It was not expected, but needed and appreciated.

Placed several items in newspaper to sell. Sold a lawn mower for $25.00. This paid for the fuel to pick up Caleb and Donna at the airport. Earlier in the year, Caleb won a trip to Portland to represent Tennessee and compete in the International Science Fair. His teacher (Donna) was also awarded a ticket and housing and vouchers for meals. They brought back $146.00 of the $400.00 given them for food and expenses. This money will be used for his graduation dinner and for hosting guests that are coming. Caleb placed 3rd internationally in engineering!

May 21
Received $25.00 yesterday. Refunded myself $250.00 from GoodSoil for money I spent on ministry items last month. No new contributions. We have $1,100.00 in the account.

There are bills on the way that will be paid with this money. Received a telephone bill of $23.00 yesterday and a Discover Card bill of $1,833.00 that is due June 16th. We also have a health insurance premium due in June for $680.00. There will be other items by the end of the month.

God is our Provider. I am His worker. I'll do my part. He will do His part. Help me believe, Lord.

May 22
It is Sunday afternoon. No gifts over the weekend until this morning. Daniel N. gave $27.00 cash today *(See 1/1/04)*. I know this was a gift from his own meager stores. He's been out of regular employment for four weeks. Mike Y. left two gifts with me today: a check for $500.00 and one for $1,000.00. The large one came from Dwane P. I know Dwane and his family live by faith, just as we, and that they have little. I imagine this gift came out of the last of their own personal money from their savings and the sale of their house. The other $500.00 came from a woman who has a terminal disease. Her gift comes during her life's darkest hour.

I am touched by who God is calling to give -- people with their own backs against the wall. These gifts are, therefore, the more precious, costly, and powerful. Reminds me of Elijah and the time God called up supplies from the widow with only one day's meal remaining to meet the needs of His servant. It is truly in the dark night of the soul that the beauty of His Holiness is most clearly seen.

May 25
Earlier this year, we planned a trip to Texas for the first two weeks in June, but how we can afford it now is not clear. We have not received any new donations as of 9:30 this morning. We have received new bills totaling $399.00.

May 26

I will simply go forward with the ministry until we literally cannot. If supplies are exhausted, we'll decide what to do then. I don't believe we should take on any debt because when we are taking on debt, it is more difficult to determine if we are making our own way or following His.

For today, I'll just wait and I'll trust that God will provide. May the LORD help me hold on, not say wrong things or believe lies, but to walk by faith, not sight, and to know HOW to do all the above.

May 27

We are almost out of propane for cooking. I called and placed an order for the minimum amount of propane, which will be $220.00. We received no donations in the mail today.

We leave Saturday (May 29) for Texas. The final opportunity for any gifts comes tomorrow (Friday). After that, we are away on the Texas trip for two weeks. We will return the evening of the 14th. The bank opens the next day on the 15th. Our Discover card bill is due the 16th.

We could deposit any gifts that may have been received in our absence on the 15th in order to pay bills by the 16th. Looks like we will need a minimum of $2,000.00 to $2,500.00. I am fasting through lunch today. I have placed before Him, in prayer, all the facts, the receipts due, the Scriptures, and my arguments based on His Word and Truth. The LORD will provide. I don't know, or even imagine, how, but I'm deciding to rest from worry. It is out of my hands and in His. I'll wait for Him, and I'll follow His lead until I literally cannot continue. May He help me follow through.

As Paul the Apostle learned and taught, it is when we are weakest that His strength is most made evident. We also came to understand that times of personal weakness and vulnerability were important for us and our ministry -- actually, they were required.

In late May and early June of 2004, GoodSoil reached its weakest financial point since its founding. In times past, when GoodSoil's funds were low, our family's personal savings were adequate to supply our personal needs until we might be reimbursed when the GoodSoil account was again full. This time, however, our personal funds were in the same condition as GoodSoil's.

As June began, we and GoodSoil had paid all bills on time, but both our accounts were near empty now. Barreling toward us, on June 16th, a large Discover card payment would be due, and a few days later, a second large bill would be due. Typically, funds had been available to us by month end to meet the needs of the coming month, but this time, for the first time, it appeared that they might not.

In addition to this, several events scheduled between June 1st and 14th were imminent and would incur expenses beyond the norm. Namely, we were committed to four days with a church in Colleyville, Texas. We had agreed to provide training for a Christian camp's summer staff in East Texas. Our nephew was getting married in Abilene, and we needed to visit the campus of the university our son would soon be attending in Lubbock. Immediately following those engagements, we were to return to Tennessee to welcome our friends Mark and Jill B., who would be there to help us receive our eight college-age summer interns. The interns were scheduled to arrive for the evening meal on June 16th.

Of course, all of these events required money above and beyond our usual expenses. So, during the last weeks of May, I followed Hezekiah's example of 'stripping the gold from the temple doors' by placing ads in the classifieds for everything we thought we could sell. A few items were sold, but not enough to make a significant difference in the situation. I counted the coins in my sock drawer (where I often tossed change from my pockets), emptied coins from the ashtrays of my vehicles, and deposited into our account literally every penny and nickel I found.

A week or so before our departure to Texas I had written my board of directors, whose primary duty as GoodSoil Directors is to pray along with me for GoodSoil's needs. I wrote,

"There are two deadlines that I'd like you to pray about: May 28th and June 16th. We have items that need supplies on those dates. I don't, at this point, know of any funds being sent to meet those needs. Only through special intervention will they be met. So, keep them before the Throne of Grace. As always, I expect you will keep these matters confidential. I ask this more for the sake of the testimony than for our personal privacy."

No further particulars of the prayer needs were supplied to my board. However, on the 28th of May (the day before we were to leave for Texas) we received a gift of $200.00 -- exactly what we needed to pay for a refill of our propane tank so Mom could have cooking gas! Earlier, on May 27th, two days before we were to leave on our trip, someone reminded me of the oppressive summer heat in Texas. How could I have forgotten? Our car's A/C wasn't working! I could sweat it out, and so could the rest of the family, but Joshua, being only a year old, with his cystic fibrosis, would not do as well. I felt compelled to repair the A/C, though we did not have the money. Still, I drove it to the shop on the 28th, the day before we were scheduled to leave for Texas. I had waited until the last possible day in hopes that some funds would arrive. They had not, but I went to the shop anyway.

May 28
"Thirty-three dollars," said our mechanic, Slim.

$33.00 was his original estimate for the air conditioning repair. I didn't have $33.00, but I also could not take Josh into the Texas heat without it. It had to be fixed. So, I approved the repair. A few minutes later, Slim delivered some bad news. "You've got some more problems." Sparing the details, the total quickly reached an estimate of $200.00! I drove to town to see if I could find the parts any cheaper than those the mechanic had, and I did. This saved me a few dollars, but one of the belts that needed replacement would have to be ordered. The mechanic said we could "chance it" on the trip. This was not comforting in the face of a 2,400 mile drive ahead of us, but we had no other choice. Another needed part was severely worn, and the mechanic strongly suggested we replace it. As the mechanic started to replace it, he discovered that the parts supply company had delivered the wrong one! By this time, the parts supply shop was closed. It was Friday. We had to leave the next morning. So, lacking another option, we were forced to take our chances with the worn original.

As the mechanics worked on the van, I sat in the adjacent waiting room. There, in the company of used tires, a greasy desk, and an often used (seldom washed) coffee maker, I took my receipts and laid them on the floor at my feet -- like Hezekiah laying the letter from Sennacherib before God. No other person was in the room as I prayed softly, but audibly,

"God, I don't know what to do here. I want to please You. I don't want to go ahead of You by taking on debt when I should not. I just don't know what else to do right now. Lord, I am willing to follow, but I am not clear on this one. I think it is important to take care of Josh, and I think it is important to meet my obligations in Texas. I need You to pay for these repairs. They say it will be $200.00. I don't have it, but You do. If You are willing, help me."

The repairs took almost an hour and a half, but an hour into that process my friend, Daniel N., drove up to the garage. It was surprising to see him since he lives 30 miles away. I thought perhaps he'd come to look at a house I'd told him was for sale in Jellico.

"Come to see that house?" I opened.
"No. I done seen it," Daniel replied. "No. I come for

another reason."

Actually, he'd been looking for me in town and was about to give up when he thought he'd try one last place -- Slim's Garage.

"How did you find me out here?" I asked. (Slim's Garage is a mile outside of town.)

"Well, I thought the other day you'd said something about getting your van ready for the trip, and I guessed you might be here at Slim's."

Daniel N. is a mountain of a man. A metal worker by trade, he's tall, barrel-chested, and massively strong. He's also slow talking, gentle natured, and generally a quiet man -- though he'll share a tale or carry on an animated discussion when spoken to. Daniel keeps life simple and finds contentment easier than most. He was driving a vehicle that needed more attention than mine the day he drove up to Slim's Garage looking for me.

After a few minutes of cordiality and chit-chat, he drew a tattered billfold from his hip pocket. The wallet was more a flap of cloth than a proper purse for one's money, but from it he slid out several bills and rolled them quickly.

"This is for you. The Lord has put it in my heart that I ain't been tithing like I should, and I felt I should bring it to you."

I was humbled. Except for occasional work, Daniel had been unemployed for almost a year. Yet today, he was God's vehicle of provision for us. It again reminded me of those Biblical stories of widows with drops of oil and of children with bread slices and minnows. I received his gift and thanked him. We visited maybe another ten minutes and then he left for home. I stepped back into Slim's waiting room.

Shortly, my van was ready. He figured my bill. I held my breath. When the unavailable parts were deducted from his original estimate, the price had dropped. He handed me a bill for $140.00. Daniel's gift? Yes, you have probably guessed. That big ole mountain of a man, moved by the gentle nudge of God's whisper in his heart, had handed me exactly $140.00. Was it God? Who else? How else?

I can't imagine that Slim had ever handed anyone a bill that brought them so near to tears of joy and shouts of praise as on that day.

Reaching home, I discovered God had been working there too. Donna told me that Kim G., a friend who lives almost an hour's drive away, had visited and left a gift of $260.00 along with some specific instructions: $200.00 was for our travel expenses (Having purchased the tank of propane with our last $200.00, this replaced that money and was timely as we began our travel to Texas.) Kim G. further specified how the remaining $60 was to be used, but I will talk more about that in a few paragraphs.

Okay, let's move to the day we left for Texas with the A/C on high! It was June 1st and our adventure was underway. For the next two weeks God supplied food, fuel, housing, and other supplies in just the right amounts and at just the right times. We never had excess, but we never lacked any necessity. We were always able to join in and even contribute to the events of our friends and family without appearing to be in any need. As far as anyone knew (or knows until they may someday read the account as it is written here) we were living with a bank account filled with cash. I will confess that those days, though a blessing, were stressful for me. At every opportunity, I stole moments away from the crowd to pray. My worry and restlessness revealed to me how faithless I could be when things were truly out of my hands. Admittedly, my wonderful wife was better at this than me, yet in spite of my weakness -- or perhaps because of her faith -- God never failed, even once, to supply what was needed.

We completed the training of the Camp Deer Run summer staff on our first stop, and they sent us off with a gift of money they'd collected among themselves. It was a fragrant offering coming from those college kids who gave out of their joy for the encouragement and training we'd brought them. When I'd agreed to come, the camp management had offered to cover our fuel expenses -- which they did. They had not offered, and I had not requested, any fee or other assistance from them, but that young staff had been nudged to help us, and their joy in doing it gave us more than cash... they gave us a fresh reminder of God's nearness and of His caring heart.

Next, in Colleyville, Texas, we met with and encouraged the Mid-Cities Church and our hosts, West and Lori S. On the night we arrived, Lori was throwing West a surprise birthday party, and she graciously invited us to join them. Actually, I tried to politely avoid the situation by suggesting that we didn't want to break in on their special day, but they insisted we join them. The restaurant was quite elegant, and considering we had seven mouths to feed in our family, the elevator ride became a barometer of the panic rising in my gut as we lifted higher and higher above the Dallas cityscape. How would we manage to pay for this? I refrained from revealing that we could not afford such an extravagance until Lori said, "Now, this is our treat. It is part of West's birthday gift to have you here." Whew! The clouds parted, and I immediately saw that God was right there with us. He was very near, very involved. Why had I imagined otherwise? Little faith, again. Well, that evening, though paupers, we dined like kings and queens on top of Dallas. Only a living God could manage that sort of thing for His subjects, only a loving God would arrange it for them, and only a merciful God would go ahead and give it to them when they so little deserved it.

On our final evening with West and Lori, I needed to drive back to the camp to get our son Daniel. He was on staff there, but had gotten permission to miss a few days to attend the wedding and visit the college campus. It was a two-hour drive to the camp, and of course two more hours back. The fuel costs would dig deeply into the gift we'd received from the camp staff, but to my complete surprise, as I walked to the door to leave, West said, "Hey Steve."

I turned toward him as a set of car keys sailed across the room. I caught them. "Take Lawson's little pickup. It hardly ever gets used, and I need it to be on the road for a while to blow it out. It is full of gas. Just use it." Wow.

Once I was out of Dallas and driving in the rural areas outside of the city, I switched off the A/C and lowered the windows. The warm, rich Texas wind ripping through the cab felt alive and vibrant on my skin. I needed that physical realness, like a pinch, to prove this was no dream, because what I'd lived the past few days was almost surreal. The living God had more than once supplied at just the right moment, in just the right way, and beyond what I could have imagined. Not only was the fuel now paid, but also our elderly van of over 225,000 miles was spared the extra wear. What could be next?

The following afternoon, we arrived in Abilene and joined the festivities of the extended family gathered for an exciting wedding event. Nieces and nephews had all grown. Aunts and uncles caught up on the months or years since last seeing one another. Loads of young friends of the bride and groom scurried busily about, attending to a variety of very important matters. Remember Kim G. -- the lady who gave $260.00 the day before we left, with specific instructions on how we were to use it? It is here that the $60.00 portion of her gift resurfaces in our story. She'd asked that this $60 be used to buy a special dress for Hannah. The specificity of her dress request seemed odd to us until we arrived in Abilene and Hannah was asked to be a part of our nephew's wedding reception -- for which she would need a special dress that matched the wedding colors! We were relieved to know the $60.00 had been given in advance, but when about to pay for the dress, an aunt insisted on buying it. That left us the $60.00. Later, we learned that one of our sons needed special shoes for the wedding. The price of the shoes was... I'm not lying... $60.00! What could have been uncomfortable, embarrassing, or downright humiliating was none of those. God had been watching out for every detail. At no point was it necessary that I reveal our financial straits. God provided at just the right moments to meet every need, protect our and our hosts' dignity, and prove Himself faithful.

We stayed in Abilene after the wedding in order to visit the Lubbock, Texas campus of Daniel's future college. The round trip drive from Abilene to Lubbock is five hours. Our plan was to visit with the admissions staff and financial aid people, and then visit a former missionary colleague from our years in Kenya before returning to Abilene in the evening. As always, I prayed a good bit about our elderly vehicle, though so far, the belts and other borderline parts had performed without a problem. After breakfast, as Daniel and I were walking to the door to leave for Lubbock, my brother-in-law, Kelly, surprised me when he said, "Hey Steve, take the Bronco. There is a tank of gas already in it." The Lord again kept miles off our old van and covered the fuel costs of a lengthy trip. Amazed by His provisions, I smiled inside and enjoyed the flat scorched earth between Abilene and Lubbock. Okay. Maybe 'enjoyed' is an exaggeration for that part of Texas, but the trip was nonetheless a joyful one as I sailed along, windows down, letting Texas' warm breath again assure me it was all very real.

Meanwhile, the looming responsibilities and associated impossibilities of June 16th were racing toward us. If the Discover card bill and the costs of hosting eight summer interns were not pressure enough, there was a third 'only-possible-through-God' matter at play. During the travel through Texas, I had come to sense that in addition to God's provisions for us, for GoodSoil's regular expenses, and for the eight interns provisions for the five weeks they were scheduled to live with us, I should ask God to deliver these provisions "in such a way as to build the interns' faith." I'd had a similar thought (nudge?) before at Camp Deer Run and God had answered. So, I began the additional request, "LORD, provide in such a way as to build the faith of my young interns."

After two weeks on the road, we arrived home on June 14th around 8 p.m. Mark and Jill B., who'd graciously offered to help us, had arrived a few hours ahead of us and already had a meal in the works. Just about the time we settled down to relax and visit, to our complete surprise, around 10 p.m. I noticed headlights coming down our drive. It was the interns! They were not scheduled to arrive until the next day around 5 p.m.! In candid honesty, my first thought was, "How will we feed them for an additional two meals?" Uncorking from their car after the sixteen hour drive from Texas, they excitedly explained, "Oh, Mr. Meeks. We made the whole trip in just one day. We hope it is okay. We just couldn't wait!"

I understood such youthful enthusiasm -- having enjoyed some of it myself at one time. Certainly, it was okay; what would two more meals mean, anyway? We had canned goods in our pantry and a freezer of beef from the calf we'd raised the previous fall. When that was gone? Oh well. It wasn't gone yet. So we welcomed them with open arms and a spread table. The interns early arrival would prove to be more than a coincidence.

The next day, June 15th, we, the interns, and Mark and Jill enjoyed a leisurely breakfast. Everyone was sitting around getting acquainted, laughing at the interns' jokes, and finishing up the meal, when around 10 a.m. the postal service called to inform me they'd left a large trash bag full of mail on our porch. This was unusual for two reasons: the postal service delivers mail to us around noon, and mail is always left up at our mailbox and not down the drive to our house. If an item is too large, we typically receive a yellow notice slip in our box informing us to pick it up at the post office, but they had actually called us this time to tell us it was out on our porch. I looked outside, and there it was. I brought the large black plastic bag full of mail in and started sorting through the contents. In two weeks' time, a lot of mail can pile up.

Before I go farther, it is important to insert a final piece of this amazing account that I have not mentioned. In the life of George Müller, on a few exceptional occasions, he made very specific requests of God. They were so specific as to not only request specific sums of money, but even to ask that specific individuals be moved to donate. Müller would ask God to nudge a specific individual to contribute a specified amount. Of course, when these individuals obeyed their 'nudge' from God, needs were met in dramatic ways, and their obedience then supplied the rest of us with a doubly-sure witness of God's readiness to hear and answer prayer. Müller did not practice magic. His specific requests were nothing like the evil use of spiritual power that attempts to coerce persons to do one's own wishes. No. In these instances, Müller brought specific names before God out of obedience to God. For it was God who put the entire thing into motion, and it was God who wanted the request made in this very name-specific way. Müller's name-specific prayer was itself an act of obedience.

So, in late May, it seemed to me that God would have me ask that GoodSoil be on the mind and heart of a particular family -- the Goodman family. I obeyed and began making this appeal to the Lord, though it had never been my practice before. Furthermore, I sensed the Lord wanted me to ask Him to move them to give $10,000.00. They had donated to GoodSoil in the past, but their practice had been to send a gift near the end of December. This was mid-June.

Making this specific-name, specific-amount request was new to me. It was also nerve-racking. To make a generic, "Lord, help us," request was far less 'dangerous' than this very specific one, because it left no room for excuses. A prayer this specific would prove that either God was involved, or *He was not.* If the Goodmans responded exactly as requested, it was an act of God. If the Goodman family sent a $10,000.00 gift before June 16th it would clearly be beyond circumstance. To ensure that this be totally a God-act, I told no one -- not even Donna. Certainly, she was aware that we were in a critical time financially because we had pinched pennies together for the past several weeks, but she knew nothing of the specific amount I was requesting or the deadline of the 16th, and above all, she knew nothing of my prayer that God nudge the Goodman's specifically.

Obviously, much of this is subjective. My 'nudges' were not a thundering voice from the sky or delivered by a shining angel with a 'thus sayeth the Lord.' And I cannot easily describe what I do mean by 'nudges' except that they are a thought that carries a deep sense of coming from beyond myself. Often, they are things I would not choose to do. I just sense that they are what God would have me to do. Avoiding or ignoring them leaves me with a sense of disobedience.

Not wanting to influence the outcome of any of this, I documented this in my journal entries, but kept quiet. I felt this put the matter in the safest place while strategically positioning for what could be powerful evidence that God is close and listening. Knowing this, you will understand my reaction when, sorting through the mailbag the morning of June 15th, I turned up a letter with the Goodman's address on it! I literally gasped so loudly and abruptly that the interns and my family, who had been chattering away, stopped to see if I was okay. Simultaneously, my mouth flew open, and my hand holding the envelope flew up. I caught Donna's eye. She asked, "What's the address?" This was unusual since most people would have asked, "Who is it from?" I told her the city on the address. She stepped over to my side and asked, "Are you going to open it?"

I remember feeling physically weak at that moment and thinking, "I am afraid to." This was holy ground… or it wasn't. The letter might contain a very wonderful gift of $50.00, and that would be a blessing, but where would it leave me in regards to my specific requests? On the other hand, what if the letter contained a gift of $10,000.00? It would be as if God Himself had walked into the room. It would mean He'd been as near as a breath. I didn't know if I was entirely ready to deal with either of those outcomes. Either way, in a moment, my life would be profoundly affected; I knew it, and the prospect of it was dizzying. Though I'd specifically asked God to move them, seeing the Goodman's address on the letter was a bit of a shock because even though I was hopeful for some sort of provisions, I honestly had not been sorting through the bag looking for a letter from them. But when I read their name on the address, I bolted up before I could even think. I cannot recall a time that I have ever had a similar reaction to anything. I don't remember what I said between telling Donna the address and her walking to my side, but I believe it was something to the interns -- who were transfixed by this mysterious behavior of their hosts -- about this being a 'God moment.'

I opened the envelope, and inside was this short note: "Our prayers are with you." Accompanying the note was a check to GoodSoil. It was for $10,000.00! Donna and I gasped, and then she squealed! We cheered! We hugged! A flood of emotion poured over the dam as I shared with everyone the details of the last weeks of exceptional weakness and total dependence upon the Lord. They listened, mesmerized. When the last drop of the story slipped over the dam, we all bowed on our knees, in stunned silence and humility, and worshipped Him. After worshipping, I realized I needed to rush to town and make a deposit. If I hurried, our Discover card payment might arrive by the one o'clock deadline on the 16th! When I asked the postal clerk when it would arrive if we used overnight service, he said it was guaranteed to arrive by noon the next day. I sent it overnight, and our payment reached Discover on time. After more than five years of being His proving grounds, we had not failed to pay a bill on time or incurred any debt personally or as a ministry. God always provided in a timely fashion.

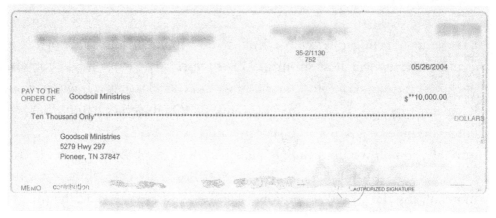

35-2/1130
752

05/26/2004

PAY TO THE ORDER OF   Goodsoil Ministries

$**10,000.00

Ten Thousand Only***

DOLLARS

Goodsoil Ministries
5279 Hwy 297
Pioneer, TN 37847

MEMO   contribution

AUTHORIZED SIGNATURE

[Check to Goodsoil for 10k]

But what about those interns? Remember, they had arrived a day early. When that mailbag arrived they were supposed to be 500 miles away instead of in my living room. They were scheduled to arrive in time to hear the story of my historic gasp, and not the actual gasp itself. They were not supposed to be enjoying a breakfast we had no budget for, but at which God would provide $10,000.00. Why had they come early? I believe it was so that they might witness the divine events of that morning. I believe it was so God might encourage me to heed His nudges, and especially when He nudges me to pray, "Do it in such a way as to build the faith of my interns!"

There was more. The following day, I was stunned to learn that Donna had also secretly been making *the exact same appeal* for weeks! She too had sensed that she should pray for the Goodmans to give $10,000.00! Neither of us had any suspicions that the other was asking the same thing!

But there was still more! I will not be surprised if, at this point, some of you may reach a point of disbelief. For me, however, here is where the evidence reached the point that **I could in no way** consider any of this an accident.

It is, for me, the crown jewel of this account -- the greatest personal benefit I've received from these entire 20 years of trusting for provisions. Two days after the letter and check arrived, Donna shared with me that Hannah, our 12-year-old daughter, told her she'd prayed and fasted for two days "for the Goodman family to send $10,000.00." That was her exact prayer! Though none of the three of us knew the others were praying it, God had nudged each of us to make the same specific request. We do not pray on a regular basis in such specifics as we did on this occasion, though we do regularly pray about every GoodSoil Ministry need with the confidence that He is listening and answering. It was a unique moment, and we obeyed, as we believed we should. As a result, the bills were paid, my interns were blessed, my daughter formed a great confidence in God as a prayer-answering God, and you now have this encouraging testimony to boost your own confidence in Him.

August 22
A note from Mark B., one of my board members, arrived today with a check that had been handed to him a few days ago. In the note he explained that he had shared the testimony about God's provisions through the Goodmans with the church where he attends. Afterwards, a lady was so moved that she approached him and handed him a $500.00 contribution for GoodSoil.

November 19
We have not taken a November salary. It is Christmas-shopping time, and this December is Donna's family gathering in Ohio. Though we hope to receive some extra personal gifts and some year-end gifts, these usually don't arrive until late in December or early in January, which makes it difficult to budget for Christmas shopping. So, it is looking like (and feeling like) another trip to be with family in which we are trusting for daily provisions and trying to fit in without anyone knowing how financially challenged we are at the moment. It isn't that we are ashamed or desire to keep up a façade, we just don't want

others to feel any obligation toward us or limit their celebrations based on our circumstance. Oh well, God has not failed us yet.

I realized today just how uphill this climb will be. I have second thoughts about investing in Jellico. The Allisons invited us to join them on a team to a new site in Africa. The invitation is very attractive, and it was an honor to be invited, but Mom's and Josh's care preclude a move. It is worthy to note that as we considered their invitation, the matter of ministry here did not weigh as a factor. Usually, the first question we'd have asked ourselves is, "How would our departure affect the work here?" The fact that ministry in Jellico was so little a part of the calculation causes me to wonder if our dream for Appalachia is slipping and if we can hold out until things move forward. I only know that we will remain faithful here until He acts.

December 5
I have been thinking about the notion that God chooses some for specific works. Many reject this idea. I do not personally hold to the idea that everyone has a specifically chosen work to do; however, I do believe that, occasionally, God has something that He wants done and He will direct a specific person to do that thing. The manner by which He notifies such people varies. Adam and God spoke directly with one another. Moses heard through a burning bush. David was informed through Samuel. Daniel heard from an angel. Jesus appeared to Paul on the road to Damascus, and Peter had a vision. Nehemiah had no voice, no vision, no prophet, no bush. He says in Nehemiah 7:5, *"God put it into my heart."* How did Nehemiah come to the conclusion that the thought in his heart was from God and not from his own imaginations? Nehemiah's experience discerning God's will seems to share some similarities with mine. For

example, he wrote, "I also told them about the gracious hand of my God upon me, and what the King had said to me." The King's offering of assistance to Jerusalem was taken as God's hand, and was confirmation to Nehemiah that what had been placed on his heart had originated in God's. This is how Donna and I have taken answers to our prayers. However, some rejected Nehemiah's view of the King's offer. Local leaders met him with resistance instead of celebration. *"But when Sanballat the Horonite, Tobiah the Ammonite official, and Geshem the Arab heard about it, they mocked and ridiculed us. 'What is this you are doing?' they asked. 'Are you rebelling against the king?'"* (Nehemiah 2:19). Despite their discouragement, the answer to his prayers and belief that this was God's call upon him engendered an unshakable confidence in Nehemiah that the incredibly impossible dream of rebuilding the walls of Jerusalem would be possible. He said, "The God of heaven will give us success."

I discussed this with three modern-day visionaries who have led or partnered with others in making a vision become a reality. I asked about their sense of 'calling' and what held them steady during times of doubt. Their answers were strikingly similar. First, the call came simply and in response to what they observed. They saw poverty and moved to relieve it. They saw the lost and moved to save them. In a similar way, Nehemiah saw Jerusalem in danger and disgrace and moved to protect.

Second, they all placed their dreams before God in prayer. Rustin Seaman of Vision Appalachia said he simply told God, "You show me what you want." Barbara Weaver of Appalachian Community Care said she "went to the Lord with it." Pattie Juarez with World Servants told stories of others she's known who believed in a vision and placed it before God in prayer. Nehemiah prayed and fasted.

Third, they all received a confirmation; sometimes it was via a financial gift, and at other times it was realizing the favor of an influential person. Ruston told of an individual who took a short-term mission trip with them and later sent $40,000.00 to jump start one of Appalachian Community Care's projects. In my case, in answer to a specific prayer request, I received $845.00 to register GoodSoil Ministries. Nehemiah considered the king's favor a confirmation that God was involved.

Later, during times of doubt or testing, these confirming signs supplied energy to persevere until the goal was realized. Those who do not share the same confirmation that their vision was in fact from God do not remain determined when troubles or difficulties come, but quickly abandon the effort or sell out. Nehemiah ran into a man like this in Shemaiah son of Delaiah in Nehemiah 6:10-13.

December 15

The LORD is everything to me. Without Him, I could not imagine living. The fear, the sheer weight of carrying all life's loads on my own shoulders would be too great. God gives me meaning, hope, aid, and supply. He waits for me after this life, and He is good.

This morning, I was lying in bed praying. My Joshua, three and a half now, so tiny and peaceful, was asleep beside me and I rubbed his soft warm back, pulled the covers up a little higher on his shoulders, and gently stroked his tuft of fuzzed hair. "If I love him this much..." I thought. "...Then how much does God love me?".

Life is powerful and unpredictable. It can rear up and overwhelm in a day or a moment. There are events and circumstances greater than any of us individually, even all of us collectively. We need God. I need Him. He is my strength and my place to gain perspective, draw hope, and find meaning when life is crazy and violent. More than anything, God is my future. If only for this life I have hope, I'm a fool. It is the age to come that is to be anticipated and for which we are to be prepared. In it there will be true comfort, pure love, total peace, and greatest blessings. God's loving gift of Jesus has secured this for me. This is why, both now and forever, the LORD is everything to me.

I wrote a poem about this when I was in college.

The Noble Dream

It all began a noble dream --
the noble wish of a Noble King

With Heart of Love -- pure and clean,
His dream? His wish?
To give us everything.

But came to spoil a Lesser King.
A selfish rogue in whom lived
a lesser dream.

And a heart of hate, both rude and mean.
His aim? His hope?
To take away our things.

"The choice is yours," Creator said,
"The selfish rogue
or Me instead?

But man grew wise, within his head,
and chose the rogue;
to The Lesser fled.

"Ah Ha! I've won!" the Hater said,
"This foolish man
will soon be dead!"

But when on the Heart of Love you tread,
it bleeds the more
for you instead.

Unseen, in His chamber in the sky,
The Noble King
began to cry

for the pain of all who'd die;
for those poor souls
who'd believe the lie.

So, planned the King once more a try
to save the man
'fore they all should die.

"I'll pay the price. The man I'll buy
no matter though
the price be high."

"What for man shall I trade?
What, the cost to redeem
the man I made?"

"What ransom must be paid
to save this one
unworthy the trade?"

He sighed, "I know what must be.
A life-for-a-life
will set him free."

"A Lamb -- pure, innocent, unscathed,
born not of a ewe;
It's My own Son, I'm afraid."

From Heaven's throne, the Beloved strode
to walk the earth.
No horse He rode.

He ate our food, wore a peasant's robe;
slept in caves
and along the road.

He healed the lame and those that grope.
Even the leper's skin
He lovingly stroked.

With wise words of love and living hope
He stirred our hearts --
Kept our dreams afloat.

We fell in love with the King's noble Man,
but our leaders took His life
with their wicked hands.

The hope of salvation! The King's final plan!
Spoiled once more
by foolish man.

"Oh God, How can we now stand?
Now that we've killed Your Son,
Your Chosen Man!"

"Would, oh, would we had a plan
to revive, and honor, and
love Your Man."

Cold silence fell from heaven like lead.
Man again had
refused the King's Bread.

But when on the Heart of Love you tread,
It bleeds the more
for you instead.

On that day, within Earth's bowels was read
a proclamation
by the One thought dead.

"No longer!" the King's Son said,
"Shall all men die!
For their sins I have now bled."

So, was restored the noble dream;
the noble wish
of that Noble King.

So, was done by the Son a thing
The Lesser ne'er thought
would ever be seen.

That Maker and made would in unison sing
of good and right,
of pure and clean.

That man to God might lovingly cling,
and come to be,
the noble dream that
God would be to man his everything.

I believe my understanding of the battle for me and the loving goodness of
God toward me has advanced from theory to experience since writing this
poem. One of my high school teachers once told me, "The proof of the pudding

is in the eating thereof." We have tasted, and though the path to Him has sometimes been difficult, the sweetness of the LORD has been our experience.

In the next chapter, I'll share the testimony of the largest single item contributed toward GoodSoil in our 20-year history. It came in May of 2006 in answer to specific, though secret, prayer.

2006 - GOD BUYS A BUILDING

January – May

As 2006 began, three church buildings were for sale in Jellico. At the same time it was increasingly clear to us that attempting to plant a church in our home was not culturally fitting. Locals preferred having Bible study and worship services in a 'church building.' My missions training taught me to consider the culture in which I was working.

The building best suited for our needs had come to be known locally as "The Mountain Women's Exchange." For a decade it had been owned by The Mountain Women's Exchange organization. Originally, a Church of Christ in Oak Ridge, Tennessee, had built it as a mission outreach to Jellico many decades before The Mountain Women's Exchange organization bought it.

The Church of Christ that was established had not lasted, and a decade after purchasing it, the Women's Exchange closed around 2002, the Women's Exchange sold the building to a local Church of God with plans to turn the facility it into a learning center. The learning center never opened, and in 2006, the Church of God was looking to sell the property. A "For Sale" sign stood out front for months.

Interestingly, in 2000 the Mountain Women's Exchange director had permitted me to hold weekly discussions about Jesus in one of their rooms, and the Greeks and our family had held Bible studies and Sunday assemblies in it around 2004. One of those Sunday mornings we were walking up the steps into the building when I noticed a LARGE dead rat lying on the steps! We removed it and entered. Aghast, I noticed another huge carcass down the hall! "Must have been a bad night for rats," I thought. Then, during the service, as Stephen Greek was leading songs, a third giant lumbered like a drunken sailor along the floor behind him! Everyone -- except Stephen -- sat horrified! We later learned that an exterminator had dispensed poisons throughout the building over the weekend. I guess it wasn't all bad, because no one fell asleep during services that Sunday or the following one.

[Jellico Mountain Women's Exchange]

It was now almost six years later, and the building had sat empty for at least the last two of those. I remember driving by the "For Sale" sign on the church's lawn and jotting down the realtor's number. When I called, it was actually the pastor who answered. He informed me that their asking price was $85,000.00 and that they'd had an offer already of $70,000.00, but they'd prefer another church get it if possible. I immediately arranged a conference call with my board of directors. Our discussion was positive and they were enthusiastic, but GoodSoil did not have the money. Someone suggested that a newsletter be sent out to 'inform people' of our plans and ask their prayers. I was glad when Stephen Greek spoke up and reminded us that since this ministry is one that relies on prayer alone, an informative newsletter seemed to go contrary to GoodSoil's principles. We all agreed not to send the newsletter, or even ask for prayers, but instead to keep the matter private and enter into prayer ourselves.

We made a simple plan: Offer the church $65,000.00. If they accepted, then let them know we did not have the money but would begin praying, with fasting by some of us, for two weeks. Then, if/when God supplied, we would buy the facility. In the meantime, the owners were not obligated to hold the facility for us -- if they got another offer they were under no obligation to us.

Though our plan seemed far-fetched, it was faithful to the only-through-prayer policy of GoodSoil. The following day I explained our offer and terms to the pastor. He took it to his church board and a few days later we sat together. They responded, "We accept your offer of $65,000.00. We also, though it is a bit unusual, accept your proposal to pray for the provisions." I clarified that ,if they felt compelled to sell to anyone else before we brought them money, they were free to sell without obligation to us.

This is the 'Letter of Intent' I handed to the pastor and his church board:

A Letter of Intent

Presented to the board of directors of the Jellico Church of God and The Hometown Mission from the board of directors of GoodSoil Ministries, inc. on January 22, 2006.

GoodSoil offers this letter of intent to enter into a season of prayer and subsequently purchase the building and grounds formerly owned by The Mountain Women's Exchange for a sum of $65,000.00 providing the following:

1. The Jellico Church of God and The Hometown Mission board accept GoodSoil's offer.
2. The funds are supplied to GoodSoil before another buyer purchases the property.

GoodSoil's board of directors offers this letter of written intent to:

1. Enter into a special season of prayer with fasting for a period of two weeks beginning January 21, 2006. During which time, we will petition God to guide these matters by His action or inactions. The resultant testimony will be confirming to both boards of directors.
2. Set aside funds, which may be delivered to GoodSoil as a result of our prayers, until the full $65,000.00 is collected.
3. Upon receipt of the full amount, GoodSoil will notify O. B. (the pastor), as the representative of the Jellico Church of God and Hometown Mission board of directors, and complete the purchase of the property, provided it remains available.

GoodSoil Ministries board of directors in no manner holds The Jellico Church of God and The Hometown Mission board of directors under any obligation to forego legitimate offers of purchase by other buyers, with the exception of any personal or corporate conviction.

GoodSoil will accept the outcome of these matters as guidance by and the reply of God in answer to our prayers and fasting.

This document was then signed by the GoodSoil board of directors and the Hometown Church's leadership.

My board and I began praying. Some also fasted. Two weeks passed with no additional donations. Then three. Four. No donations.

Certainly, one could argue, "How could there be any response, since no one knew?" But this would not be accurate. In fact, someone did know, and He was the only One who needed to know. Meanwhile, we waited in silence and watched for His response.

One night, during this waiting time, I drove passed the building and saw lights on inside. The pastor was showing it to someone -- my heart sank. The prospect of someone else owning the building did not affect me, but the loss of the exciting possibility that God might actually do this impossible thing would be a disappointment. On the other hand, if God did it; if we had actually discerned rightly; and if God would be moved by our prayers, then what a powerful testimony to others and what an affirmation of our ministry that would be!

About four weeks after the GoodSoil board's time of special prayer, Todd, a friend from Nashville, called. "Hey, Steve. There is someone here in Nashville who wants to meet you and hear about GoodSoil."

That same weekend Todd and his friend came to see us. A tall older gentleman was introduced to me as Bob. "Tell me about GoodSoil," Bob asked. It took about 30 minutes to explain our interest in Appalachian church planting, involvement in youth training via Mission Camps, and our interest in missionary care. He had only a few additional questions before leaving. His visit was short, but he had encouraged me by his words and show of genuine interest. "Well, I need to be heading to Nashville," Bob said. "Thank you for what you're doing. I'm very impressed and hope you'll keep it up." I thanked him and he left. That was it. We never talked about the prayer request for the building. Of course, we didn't talk about any need. We talked about things we were currently involved with and what we hoped to see happen through ministry, but never so much as a hint that we had hopes or need for a building. The following day Vince V., our coworker and the owner of an outreach vocational ministry called A Common Ground Coffee Shop, handed me a check for $500.00. "This is from Bob. He donated the same amount to the coffee shop ministry." I smiled. God had again been generous and near to both our work and those who were partnering with us in the Gospel.

About ten days after Bob's visit, while my family and I were in Ohio visiting relatives, I received a call from GoodSoil board member Mike Y. After exchanging greetings, Mike asked, "Hey, Steve, what kind of trouble have you been causing in Jellico?" I had to think. Perhaps someone has been offended? Maybe I've said something that was misunderstood? Mike quickly chuckled, "I'm just kidding. Hey, I have Bob here in my office and we would like to bring a couple of others and myself and come up there and see you. When will you be around?" We made arrangements for a meeting in Jellico in a few days. When their car drove into town, three people were inside. Mike spoke, "Steve, this is Neil. He's a friend of Bob's, and they want to take a look at a building in town." Bob had evidently done some research after his first visit, learned that Mike was on the GoodSoil board, and questioned him about the ministry. Then he proposed that Mike organize a visit. Mike continued, "Steve, Bob and Neil want to know if you can get the key to the church building down in town," Three churches were for sale in Jellico at that time. We had only prayed about one of them -- the former Mountain Women's Exchange Building. Surprisingly, it was the only one Bob wanted to see!

I contacted the pastor, and as he handed the key to me, he held up three fingers. I looked at him, waiting for an explanation. "There are three bids on the building. You'll have to decide today. We'd like you to have it, but if you can't do it today, we'll have to accept one of the others, but you are first," he said. My stomach tightened. I felt sick. The primary thing I did not want to do that day was to push or coerce those guys and spoil any testimony that might result. Should I tell them this new information or keep it to myself and wait for God lead them? I wasn't clear. So, unsure of the right move, I kept the pastor's ultimatum to myself as we toured the Mountain Women's Exchange building.

The building was not a beauty. It was cold, dank, and full of odds-n-ends, office supplies, desks, trash, and something that had died not too long ago! The stench was strong in certain rooms. The windows were tinted in amber. The carpet was dark red and very soiled. It had been built in the 60s, and the original dark brown paneling was almost claustrophobic. But I knew that cleaning, repairing, and painting the place would brighten it up and bring it to life, making it perfect for our ministry.

After a look at the church, I took Bob, Neil, and Mike on a quick drive through the area, and then ordered lunch at A Common Ground Coffee Shop. All morning, I had been in a mental tug-of-war struggling over whether to tell Bob and Neil about the pastor's deadline. At lunch, I concluded that if I were in their shoes, I'd want all the facts. So, I told them what the pastor had told me about the deadline. Neil abruptly jumped to his feet. "Bob, we need to go for a walk and talk." Without another word, the two left the table and stepped outside. Mike and I sat in stunned silence. "What was that?" I asked. Mike chuckled, "I don't know."

About 15 minutes later, Bob and Neil returned in good spirits. "Hey guys, this has been a great morning with you. Lunch is on us." They paid for lunch and we shared farewells.

That was it. No indication of why the sudden exit or what they'd discussed. I, of course, wondered if I'd blown it by mentioning the pastor's time frame but knew my motives had been only in their best interest. I had peace and drove home. There were still eight to ten hours left in the day. Anything might happen, so I delayed giving the pastor any answer. My phone rang. It was Mike. "Steve. We are almost back to Nashville, but these guys wanted me to give you a call. They have talked with me all the way here and decided that they want to get you that building." There it was! As matter-of-fact as you please. When God is in it, a mountain is lifted as easily as a feather. Still in a fog of disbelief, I called my board and then informed the pastor, "God has supplied the money, Pastor. We will be making arrangements with you soon. We are buying the building."

Two weeks later Bob, Mike, and I met at a Wendy's restaurant near our county seat of Jacksboro. He handed me the receipt showing where he and Neil had paid $65,238.25. He also produced a copy of a lease agreement we'd been discussing over the phone. They had decided to lease the building to us for $1 a year. We, in turn could use it for the next five years in any way we wished, so long as we insured it and paid property taxes. All of us would reassess after that. "Perfect!" I thought, "God supplied GoodSoil with the tool we requested, and in such a way as to leave a powerful testimony."

Cleanup and remodeling of the building over the ensuing years produced an additional series of inspiring testimonies involving literally hundreds of stories of God nudging people to come to our aid. For example, the first week we had control of the property, a church group from Texas arrived with no funds but eager hands. At that point, we needed muscle and lots of arms and legs to clear out the old desks, rip up the rotting carpet, and wash down the walls. It was absolutely perfect for the group and GoodSoil. With the building cleared of clutter, we would need to paint and begin remodeling. A few days before the Texas group completed their work, a youth group whose planned mission trip had fallen through contacted me. They had heard of us somehow (God? Certainly!) and wondered if they could help us. Sure! They asked for specific ideas of what they could do. I asked if they could help us paint and remodel the entry and hallway. They thought that was something they could do, though I wondered to myself, "How are we going to pay for the paint and materials?" I did not ask for their financial assistance or indicate that we needed funds to purchase materials. The day before their arrival the youth pastor called me again. "Hey Steve, I forgot to mention to you that we will be bringing about $1100.00 to help with supplies." It was perfect! Just how perfect would be realized upon their actual arrival. Their group was small in numbers and size, consisting of just 11 junior high kids and their youth pastor -- but he happened to have been a finish carpenter! I am not kidding you. Without a single public or private announcement or appeal, people from around the country began supplying everything we needed, from trash cans, to toilets, to audio visual equipment, to furniture, to internet service.

Several months after building renovations had begun, Jennifer, a lady familiar with our ministry, asked, "Steve, how could I help you? How about an office for your counseling?" A month later, while I was away on a mission trip to Africa, she and four other women secretly remodeled, decorated, and furnished one of the rooms, turning it into a counseling room and office. The first Sunday after my return from Africa -- before I'd had a chance to see it for myself -- one of the men asked if he could see the newly decorated office.

As I opened the door, my jaw dropped. The congregation, who had followed behind us, broke into applause at the reveal! The ladies had done the work without telling me! Now, it was totally transformed and ready for me to begin providing local Christian counseling.

Though Jennifer's case is an exception, something that I have noticed, looking back over the years, is how few people asked if I wanted their help. The large majority of things were done without asking my permission. I was never asked "Do you need Wi-Fi? or "Would you like to have a big screen TV installed in your classroom for presentations?" The sanctuary stage was modified; utensils and food service items were supplied; furniture, desks, and office equipment just appeared as the LORD prompted individuals and organizations. The lawn was mowed for us. Janitorial equipment, supplies, and cleaning were all taken care of without a word (or permission) from me. All the while, money for utilities, taxes, and insurance was always supplied in time. So, it begs the question, "How?" It's a strain to manage almost any operation of this size even with a large budget, a staff, and some type of management system; yet during these years, God Himself was the Supplier and the Manager of all these matters for us.

Freedom from these details allowed me to attend to ministry concerns. Thousands of hours of worship, teaching, encouragement, fellowship, counseling, training, and praying, along with buckets of tears and loads of laughter, flowed within those walls over the next nine years. A Celebrate Recovery program that was recognized and awarded by the county Chamber of Commerce was launched there and held weekly recovery meetings there for eight years before relocating in 2014. Media Mission Camps were hosted in the renovated facility for three summers. World Servants, the missions training organization, used it for almost a decade as a training base from which to serve GoodSoil and the community. The Jellico Community Church would be birthed there and eventually disseminate into the community from its auditorium. I would provide Christian counseling at the building beginning in 2012, and Springs of Life Recovery Center would further remodel the building in the last half of 2014 and open a men's recovery center on January 1st, 2015.

I compare the overall experience of these years of prayer and trusting and witnessing God's provisions to that of a bag being filled with small pebbles; some small, some a little larger, but none individually very heavy. However, as their numbers increase, the collective weight grows. Likewise, collectively, what has happened here cannot be dismissed as inconsequential; something very unique has occurred that leaves us with weighty evidence that God indeed hears and answers prayer.

[Meeks Family in 2006]

2011 - THE LARGEST CASH DONATION

June 30

I'm fast-forwarding five years to the events of June 30th, 2011, when I sent a mid-year report to my board of directors. An exciting portion of that report is copied for you here:

Other good news is the most recent testimony given to the world through GoodSoil. As of the last day of May this year, we had not received a personal salary payment for the year; neither had our fuel for the year been reimbursed, nor had our health insurance benefit been paid.

However, only two days later, on June 2nd, we were able to be reimbursed year-to-date for the fuel and health insurance benefit, although our salary remained outstanding. Three days after that, on June 5th, I made the following entry in my journal: "I expect the LORD will move the Goodmans to send the $10,000.00 they have sent every June for several years now, but I'm asking Him to move them to send $15,000.00 - $20,000.00 this year." It was an uncomfortable request, but one that I sensed that God wanted me to make.

Apparently, the day after I obeyed what I sensed to be God's wish, Mrs. Goodman was moved to make a donation to GoodSoil. Her gift arrived June 9th with a note. The note read, "Steve and Donna, you continue to be an inspiration to us. Your love for the people of Jellico is making an eternal difference and your prayer on their behalf is calling His Kingdom to that place. Praise the Lord for His work through you." Enclosed was a check for $15,000.00!

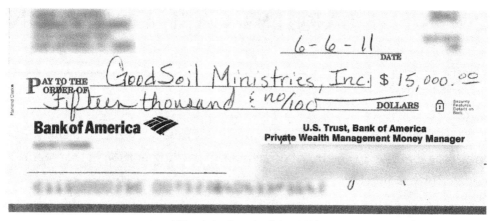

[Check to Goodsoil for 15k]

On June 28th, I got phone calls from both Todd A. and Phil D. of Priest Lake Fellowship Church. The church had taken a special collection for missions last Sunday, and devoted their entire service to prayer for missions. Every member was permitted to 'ear mark' the mission they wanted their donation to assist. It was made clear and announced several times leading up to the day of collection and again on that day that PLCF has no financial responsibility with the work in Jellico and that we have ONLY requested their prayers. However, $1750.00 was donated to GoodSoil anyway.

The outstanding salary due me through the end of May was $16,250.00. The Goodman's gift covered all but $1250.00. The gift from PLCF paid the remainder, leaving a surplus of $500.00 in the GoodSoil account. In just 11 days, between June 2nd and June 12th, God supplied $20,550.00. We are delighted by His care.

As I'm working through the edit of this section, it is 2017. The $15,000.00 gift from the Goodman family remains the largest cash donation ever made to GoodSoil. Only the purchase and subsequent use of the Mountain Women's Exchange Building was a larger financial investment in our ministry.

2016 - THE PEOPLE

A full 20 years have passed since leaving Kenya. Two questions cause me to reflect today: How did the time go so quickly, and what has happened as a result?

The first is the easier. The time went quickly because we were busy, and it went quickly because looking back is always a shorter view of time than looking ahead. Some of those days, and especially those nights, were long, long, long. I often wondered if we'd make it financially. Many times I questioned my decision to live in Appalachia. I confess that I often daydreamed of being somewhere else, doing something else. I know that those days and seasons seemed long only because of my mindset. A worrying, doubting, anxious person's hours drag along. I confess my guilt in all three of those categories. This hasn't been an easy journey, though I'm sure that it could have been if I had been of a different mind -- the mind that Christ had. I wasn't a perfect candidate for the job in most ways, but I suppose my adventuresome, strong, faithful, faith-filled, dear wife and I were willing enough that God included us. We are so, so, so delighted that He did.

I think the second question deserves a more thoughtful response. What has happened as a result of our time and effort here? I'll answer in two parts. First, I'll share a summary of what we've experienced, seen, and come to know. Second, I'll let you hear from some of the people who've been affected over these years.

So, what have been the results of our work? I can't tell you everything. Not that I don't want to share, but I just don't know all that's come from the overnight or multiple night stays of over 5000 individuals. I do know they've all dined richly! (My wife is an amazing cook! I mean a-m-a-z-i-n-g.). And I know they've seen hospitality that is open-handed and genuine. I know they've been taught, trained, entertained, prayed for, prayed over, heard, held, helped, handled without judgment, and offered hope. I know they've seen Jesus' ways and been placed near Him among the poor, with the downcast, and in the company of the sinner and the Pharisee. I know that labor in the LORD is not unproductive. Without knowing specifics, I am confident that much, very much fruit has resulted.

There are a few general outcomes that I know with certainty, however. Some of those we've trained or encouraged through our mission camps, internships, and apprenticeships have served in foreign mission points. Germany, Mozambique, Togo, Kyrgyzstan, Libya, Uganda, Rwanda, Tanzania, Kenya, China, Haiti, the Dominican Republic, Honduras, Guatemala, Mexico, and Canada are a few I can quickly recall. Points in the United States are too numerous to list. The number of disciples resulting from their efforts is exponentially larger than those realized here in Appalachia.

We've hosted churches and individuals from a wide swath of denominations. Baptist, Methodist, Churches of Christ, Nazarene, Churches of God, Catholic, Seventh Day Adventist, Afro-Centric, Community, House Church, and Mega-Churches have all been welcomed and treated with an equal love. To none have we hesitated to share what was true and in their best interest. I don't know of anyone who left us angry, bitter, or hurt. God's ways brought restoration, healing, and unity.

There are individual cases that I recall, like the teen from Texas who was so closed and rebellious while with us, but whose heart was changed after leaving. He then returned to our place, which he considered the birthplace of his faith, to be baptized in our creek. I think of Jerry, our intern, and his friends from the University of Texas, who bounced in here so full of laughter and a kind of rich-rawness in their faith. I am also reminded of the gentle-spirited Linda who sought respite in our home after serving in China and who is now a member of an active missions committee in a large Nashville church. And how can I forget Brandon and Ben, who pursued military careers as members of elite forces in the Army and Marines? There was also the telephone-coaching of a zealous, evangelistic freshman college student in California needing advice on the practice of personal disciplines or on disciple-making among his fellow students. There is the exceptionally gifted young man whose identity must be kept anonymous because he serves incognito in a hostile culture, in constant danger, to serve Christ in secrecy and obscurity even to this hour, and Curt, the Scotland missionary candidate whose intense phobia of flying was completely lifted from him after a single season of praying together.

There have also been a number of couples who met here; and those who married here. There have been the engineers, and the poets, and the singers, and the entrepreneurs; the popular, the funny, the timid, the shy, the humble; and the many, many foreign nationals who came for a drink, or a meal, or just to see, but always to leave enlightened by the glory of God.

But here are a few stories I know very well, and I want you to hear them:

Derek and Sarah

Derek was in his early 30's. His wife, Sarah, was in her 20's with two small children. They were traveling a rocky road, but over the few months leading up to our initial contact with them, God had been working in their hearts during a season of repentance and change. We first met them almost a decade ago this year. For Donna and me, it had come after eight long, hard years of a very modest production after an epic effort in Appalachia. We had discussed many times if moving to the area had been a 'misread' of God's will for us. Yet something would not let me pull the trigger on leaving. The argument for leaving was gaining ground year after year. At least, that was the case until we met Derek and Sarah. Ironically (divinely appointed?), our first visits with them were over hot drinks at A Common Ground Coffee Shop -- which our coworkers Vince and Misty had opened in a leap of faith as a self-supporting outreach to the community. Derek and Sarah liked the shop and Vince and Misty, and they were drawn to our latest effort at a church gathering that was authentic, informal, non-traditional, and yet biblical.

Reflecting, there were a number of 'items' which created this perfect storm -- none of which was I responsible for planning. The Mountain Women's building had just been purchased by two men I'd literally only known a few hours. They had then leased it to GoodSoil for $1 a year. With a facility in hand, a procession of volunteer groups began to appear and the flow continued until the building was cleaned and furnished. Meanwhile, Vince, Misty, Donna, the Greeks, and my mom began holding our Sunday worship meetings at the GoodSoil Center (our new name for the former Women's Exchange). About that same time, a group of believers from Nashville (Priest Lake Christian Fellowship) had discovered us and joined our efforts in Appalachia. When their elders heard we had decided a date for our first Sunday gathering, they (all ten of them and their families!) arranged to come the Saturday before to worship and pray in the building and invite God to bless our initial Sunday service and us. Derek and Sarah were among those who were attending that Saturday gathering with Priest Lake Community Fellowship. During that service, the perfect storm climaxed, turning our eight years of famine into more than a decade of abundance.

It was uncomfortably hot in the building that day. About 40 of us were packed into the largest room that was available for use. The PLCF group was undaunted. The local visitors appeared willing and we were, of course, just elated at the gathering. During one portion of the gathering, we were all invited to pray. Anyone could pray aloud if they wished. Several did, and then, to my left and behind me, I heard a woman's voice, "LORD, bless this young woman and the child within her." She was referring to Sarah. Early Sunday morning, Sarah called Donna. "Do you know that woman who prayed for me?" "Yes," Donna replied. "Why?"

"She prayed for the baby I was carrying, but Donna, I'M NOT PREGNANT! Do I look pregnant?" She did not look pregnant, and neither Donna nor I knew why the lady had prayed this. Later we would ask and learn that the prayer had been offered despite feeling uncomfortable about it. She told us, "I just felt like God wanted me to pray that." We counseled Sarah, "Well, IF it is God's work, then you'll have a child, but if not, then we are sure that she (Judy T.) meant no harm." A few hours later, Sarah called. "Donna! I sent Derek to the pharmacy to get one of those tests. Donna, it says I AM PREGNANT!" The next day Sarah went to the local clinic where a second test confirmed a pregnancy. News spread. People came. Our first gathering filled the smallest room. The next week we were twice as many. The third week we doubled again. Enthusiasm was mounting.

For the next three years, a Wednesday 6 a.m. Men's Bible study was held at A Common Ground Coffee Shop. Derek invited and influenced most of the men who came. We often had as many as a dozen. Within a short time, a Celebrate Recovery was launched in The GoodSoil Center. Derek was again responsible for much of its success and became the primary leader for it. Filled with the Holy Spirit, he went on to establish a non-profit charitable Christian organization which would accomplish much good in our area. God also led him to become the point man in establishing a chaplaincy for the county sheriff's department.

Through Sarah, interest in homeschooling increased and a co-op sprouted to involve several local ladies and their children. She's also proved to be a skilled promoter and was key to the success of most of our church and Celebrate Recovery events. Their marriage strengthened as they sought our advice on building their family. Elijah was born, as prophesied, and joined their other two children. In 2014 they felt God's nudge to provide foster parenting and are currently in the final stages of adopting a little girl. In the fullness of time,

God put Derek and Sarah in our path. Now, a decade later, they are among the strongest in the community of faith in Jellico, but it was not a growth that came without challenges. Their house burned a few years ago. It was devastating, but Derek quickly said, "Well, things don't last. We'll be okay." Derek's job has been filled with ups and downs. Some of the greatest personal challenges of his life have been associated with employment. Derek and Sarah have faced their thorn bushes and experienced a harvest of increased righteousness as they, at every turn, have humbled themselves under God's good hand and continued to follow His ways. They built a new home and did a truly amazing job on every element of the place, but the thing that strikes me most every time I visit -- besides their children happily playing around us -- are the Scriptures they've had painted in large print on the walls of almost every room. In fact, their house is a metaphor of their new lives -- new, still under construction, full of life, full of children, and full of God's glory.

Ben and Brittany

We first met Brittany as a college student. She'd come with several nursing students and her mentor and instructor, Jennifer Hicks, on a Spring Break Mission trip to Jellico. The trip impacted the whole group such that they made it an annual retreat/mission for several seasons afterwards.

It was on one of those trips that Brittany first saw Ben at a church service. She set her sights on him right then (you'll have to get the whole story from her) and they are married today!

As I write this, Brittany is a nurse at the hospital in Jellico and Ben is Program Director for Springs of Life and completing a PhD in Christian Counseling. Their son, Beniah, was born about a year ago and is a blonde-haired, friendly delight to whom we've already laid claim for one of our granddaughters. Ben grew up in Kentucky and has an effervescent personality that meets strangers with the ease most of us have around old friends. Brittany is from middle Tennessee and brings smiles to light up any event. They are a great team together and serve quietly but are very capable leaders when called upon. They live in Jellico but worship at Cornerstone in Williamsburg, Kentucky. Ben also attends my Wednesday morning men's Bible Studies at McDonald's and has an insatiable hunger for Scripture and living out biblical manhood.

The Claytons are one of a few families Donna and I have offered to shepherd throughout their lives. We are amazed that, as gifted and capable as they are, the Claytons humbly listen to us -- even when making major decisions around career and marriage and parenting. We are honored by their partnership in the gospel and enjoy their effervescent, never-a-dull-moment friendship! Take a look at their picture and you'll see what I mean.

Tim and Hope

Hope is bright, cheerful, energetic, and committed. The first time we met was on one of those weekends when Dwane P. brought a group of families up to help us build our house. Afterwards, Hope kept coming back. She attended Africa Mission Camp and the European Mission Camp in 2001, came back for the International Camp in 2002, and was a GoodSoil intern the year following. She continued bringing others for weekend visits or ministry afterwards until 2008, when Hope moved about 20 miles from us to Williamsburg, Kentucky, working as a nanny.

In 2003, I'd met a young schoolteacher and football coach from Williamsburg. The first time I recall meeting Tim, I was impressed. As a high school senior, Tim led his father's successful state representative campaign; clearly, he was a natural leader. In fact, I told him he should be president! What got my attention, and my time, was Tim's genuine hunger for God. His family was one of strong faith, but his personal faith was just awakening and he was a dry sponge for my input into it. For eight years, we met and talked on our porch almost every week for an hour or more. Topics ranged from how to understand Scripture to how to apply truth, set goals, follow dreams, think of the future and assess the past. He had questions about romance, missions, and the will of God. Humbly and candidly, we shared the beautiful and the not-so-beautiful events of our past and present. Christ spoke into it all and Tim received His words with an open heart.

His involvement in Cornerstone Church in Williamsburg grew. Behind the scenes he was making disciples. He shared Sunday speaking duties and often led the worship portion. Tim is a talented musician and singer, but beyond this, he is the best I've ever known in his ability to lead without drawing attention, to be in front without distracting, to gently turn our disjointed thoughts from the mundane and attract us into majestic presence of God through song. It is more than a gift; it springs from whom God created him to be.

One day, out of the blue, Hope was at our house and began asking if we knew anything about the young ministry leader/schoolteacher at Cornerstone Church. Within a week of her inquiry, without having mentioned to Tim our conversation with Hope, Tim asked if I knew Hope and what I would advise him to do about getting to know her. I simply replied with my encouragement to get to know her. I never hinted at her having noticed him. Donna and I still giggle about being secretly in the middle, watching the sweet and beautiful way these two came to know one another.

I was honored to pronounce them "man and wife" in April of 2010.

Today, they have a son and a daughter. Tim is the lead pastor of Cornerstone Church, where he and Hope have led a group of about 35 members to 160+ in the past 16 months. Tim says about Cornerstone, "We are a gateway to Appalachia. Kids from the university here go back out to their Appalachian home-communities. We build on this opportunity to make disciples of them so they can in turn take it home and make disciples. We are also situated to meet the unique need of the local community. They are a forgotten people in need of discipleship."

The powerful thing about Tim and Hope is that they understand that disciple-making means personal investment in people *over a long period of time*. They know cognitively, and they know it by experience, because they've been made disciples themselves. We are delighted to serve alongside them at the Cornerstone Church as Shepherds.

Nathan and Brittney

Theirs is a story of Dorothy and Toto running from the Wicked Witch of the West, glimpsing behind the great curtain of Oz, but ends in Cair Paravel rather than back in Iowa!

(Cair Paravel, if you are unfamiliar, is the fictitious castle in The Chronicles of Narnia *from which the kings of Narnia who were under Aslan ruled. Aslan was the metaphorical equivalent of Christ.)*

I first met Nathan when he was in his late teens or early twenties. He was far from God. Over the years, his concerned and anxious grandmother often solicited my prayers and help for him. I prayed, I visited, I wrote, and I called. He remained unaltered. Nathan was a quiet rebel; the kind who tolerated the well-intended advisors, then continued his march to personal destruction. Multiple auto accidents and a near-death event did not deter him. Jail and prison terms failed to move him. Estrangement from family didn't bring remorse or change. Drugs, alcohol, and self-destruction were driving him at a fast pace along the crags of personal destruction toward the cliff of death. Nathan had a good family who gave him everything a person could want. His father was present and his mother was too. Though they loved him, I could tell from his behavior, and from his skin hidden behind tattoos, that for some reason, he didn't love himself. After so many personal attempts, my confidence in his change had lessened over the years. His pattern of remorse, return to drugs, and negative ramifications stole my belief that he would survive, let alone change. But God never gives up, even when we think all hope is lost.

When I heard Nathan was in a recovery center in Gatlinburg, TN and had 'really changed this time,' I smiled, but inwardly thought, "He won't last." Four months into his stay, he was still doing well, and Cliff, the director at our Springs of Life ministry, wanted to bring Nathan back to Jellico to become the first member of our outreach. I agreed, but honestly, I didn't think Nathan would make it a month. I was wrong. When Nathan graduated Cliff added him to our staff. After that, Nathan and I visited one-on-one weekly, and I got to know him as I had not before. This is when I got my first glimpses of his new heart. He was a different man than the one I'd known for so many years!

Getting to know the new Nathan and watching him steadfastly hold the line, seek the truth, and listen to counsel sparked a thought: "Hmmm. I wonder if this guy might be interested in Brittney."

Bubbly, energetic, all smiles, and eager for the New Life, Brittney was the effervescent mother of two boys despite also being a young widow, dealing with chronic health concerns, and being stuck in a small town. Donna and I had come to know this 28-year-old sweetheart as our friend. We had invested many hours working through the grief of losing her husband to cancer, teaching her how to rear her two young sons, and guiding her over the roadblocks and hurdles in her journey to a deeper faith. Brittney was amazing in how she emerged from these challenges with a special kind of tenacity and brightness that had us thinking, "How can we ever find a man in this small town who might come anywhere near her level of maturity in Christ?"

I invited Nathan into my office one afternoon. I simply asked if he had noticed Brittney. He had, and the idea had already crossed his mind that she might be someone he should know. I encouraged him to get to know her. He said, "Okay, Steve, but you have to help me. I want to do this right." A bit unsure at first, he stumbled nervously through their first couple of meetings but listened to my coaching. I discouraged physical touch, encouraged prayer together, and set the expectation that things should progress slowly for at least 12 months before making any big relationship leaps. He took my advice and within a few days introduced himself to Brittney. She immediately came to us and was like, "I don't know this guy! I'm not looking for anyone!" Donna and I calmed her fears by assuring her that Nathan was someone we knew pretty well and that we believed him to be a man after God's heart. We encouraged her to give him a chance until she could find out for herself what he was like. When he asked her out, she agreed to a date, and then another, and then... well, it's been over a year, and I'm scheduled to perform their wedding also.

In the meantime, Nathan befriended her two sons. He and the oldest boy (11 years old) went hunting together this year. The boy shot his first squirrel on one of their early outings, which was very special in that his biological father was a squirrel hunter. But that was just the start. Over the next eight to ten weeks, he proceeded to shoot two does and a buck!!! Nathan could have not been more proud if he'd downed those deer himself. A healthy bond is forming with the boys. Brittney is delighted. Nathan is leading. Christ is at the center of their relationship and will be at the center of their home, which is set to become a real-life version of C.S. Lewis' Cair Paravel!

Cliff and Allison

I mentioned Cliff as 'Cliff B.' earlier in this story on January 4th, 2001. Here I want to offer more about him and his bride, Allison.

Cliff is intense and serious (though he can joke and cut up too). I mean that in every positive way imaginable. What I mean is that when he is 'sold' on something, he is tenacious; when he is committed, he has a white-knuckle grip; when he is compassionate, you find both fire and water in his eyes. There is no middle ground with Cliff, and you don't ever have to doubt his word. Personally, I admire his fevered zeal for righteousness. In his zeal, Cliff is mature. He can pause, listen, balance, and pivot if it is best. Though a man of vision and dreams, he is a realist and knows how to seek the help and thoughts of others before moving on an idea. So when he came to me asking about the young physicians assistant at the clinic, I knew it was more than casual conversation.

Allison had long before gained a confidant in Donna. She had shared with us her interest in getting to know Cliff before he was aware of it himself. Their initial meeting had been by 'chance' at the clinic. It had not gone as well as might be hoped. Cliff's 11-year-old daughter was being seen and was nervous about getting an injection. Cliff had assured her that she would not be needing a shot. So when Allison noticed from her records that a vaccine was due… well, it was a strained moment. Everyone lived through it, but Cliff (and Allison) had each noticed the other.

For all the good in him, Cliff had some softening of the edges to do. Allison had to extend lots of grace. They both needed to learn a great reliance on the Lord. Oddly, some of the more 'challenging' issues in their relationship initially revolved around their faith. Both were fully committed disciples of Jesus, but from very different backgrounds. Bridging that gap was difficult, and it took a lot of work and some time to arrive on common ground and discover a comfort zone without compromising on values or truth.

It was a delight to watch and an honor to occasionally guide them as they navigated their way to love and commitment in marriage. Their ceremony was an outdoor affair at our farm on a bright and rather warm afternoon. Just before walking to the front of the assembly, the heat and the tight collar and the nerves merged as Cliff said, with all sincerity, "I think I'm going to throw up." Never have I seen this typically cool-as-a-cucumber guy so rattled. He was actually pale! The wedding was beautiful; the vows moving; the ceremony holy. God was clearly placed at the center of their relationship. They've bought an older house in Jellico and are refinishing it. I was honored to be among the first to be told when they learned that Allison was expecting! It's a blessing to know that this child will be reared in an environment of love, peace, and faith.

Trevor and Tommie Leigh

Tommie was a high school student, the first I remember meeting her. Trevor was a college student who joined in helping us with our Celebrate Recovery program. I never envisioned the two of them as a married couple, but they met and loved and married each other behind my back (just kidding!). Tommie is vivacious, the life of the party, talkative, and epitomizes an outdoorsy-tomboy-beauty-queen. She is down-to-earth practical, a teacher by profession, a homebody by nature, a servant, and one of the most hospitable young women I know. She laughs heartily and jokes easily. She tends to take on more than she should, but manages more than you might imagine she could. And, personally, I think Tommie is just plain fun to be around.

Trevor likes a party, but is quiet in a crowd. Get him one-on-one and he is an easy conversationalist. He is loyal, faithful, and dependable. He doesn't seek the limelight, but in more private circles he is known to be quite creative, multi-talented, and something of a crazed dancer! Trevor's faith is firm. He has the closet-room relationship with Jesus down pat, and it is clearly evidenced in his public service. Trevor and Tommie love life and giving life. Life is all around them. They raise a garden and chickens. They have a stray cat and a Golden Retriever puppy. They provide love and care to two foster children. So when it seemed they would not be able to create life, it was really difficult news. Prayers had been offered, lots of them, and yet, more than three years into their marriage, Tommie had not conceived.

Near the end of their first year of marriage, Trevor's coworker, Richard, told him that he believed God had shown him the couple would have difficulty conceiving, but that the LORD wanted to encourage them by letting them know that they would have a child. Richard asked if Trevor had a preference for a boy or girl. Trevor did not, but Tommie had wanted a boy. Richard said, "You'll have a boy." At that time, Tommie was studying the life of Josiah, so when Trevor shared Richard's word with her, they decided Josiah would be the name of their son, if they had one.

Afterwards, Trevor and Tommie made an appeal to their church elders for prayers, but the elders did not take immediate action. They prayed privately and sought medical counsel, but nothing changed until one evening at a small gathering of friends. We were all eating and visiting when the notion struck me that Trevor and Tommie must surely be discouraged by their inability to conceive. We had prayed for them before, but that evening, I had one of those gentle nudges that I could not ignore. It seemed the LORD would have us pray for them once again. So before the group dispersed that evening, I suggested we encircle Tommie and Trevor on our knees, place our hands on them, and offer a special, united appeal for a child. I prayed, "Lord, grant them a child, and grant that child an extra measure of Your Spirit so it will be inclined to follow You all the days of its life." That was it. We stood. Everyone hugged them. Chit-chat restarted, and before long everyone left for home. There were no thunderclaps, no voices from above, and no emotional experiences. Yet we had made our appeal, and it was before God's merciful throne. A month later, to the day, the group was again gathered for a meal when Tommie and Trevor called us to attention for an announcement. Multiple tests had confirmed they were expecting!

It's been about a year since that circle of prayer, and a few miles from where I am writing, Trevor is home with Tommie helping with their healthy baby. Tonight, they'll be bringing that precious bundle to our small group meeting. It will be my first time to meet the little guy. Yes, that's right; they have a boy, and his name is Josiah, which means, "Jehovah has healed."

Like all the many other prayer answers we've witnessed over the years, this one astounds us and lifts our hearts, but Josiah's story is not the only one like it. Stephen, Elijah, and Esther are other children who 'couldn't' be among us, but, after prayer, they are, and though children and small, they give us great reasons to dismiss our doubts, redouble our confidence, and believe afresh that God is real, that He cares, that He hears, and that He answers our prayers. The stories shared in this book are only a few of the many we have lived during these twenty-eight years. I've chosen this sampling to strengthen your confidence in God, your commitment to praying, and your responses to God's gentle, quiet nudges. If, however, you are not yet persuaded, I have a final piece that should tip the scales. Over the past twenty years, without a single word of solicitation, or so much as a hint of need, over a million dollars have been provided to our family and ministry through prayer alone -- more than a million additional pebbles of evidence! Can so many varied and numerous examples be dismissed as mere coincidence? I do not see how they can. I am convinced God has been at work providing ample proof that He is not an ancient legend, a myth, far from us, or uninvolved. If I did doubt that we serve an active and engaged God, I can no longer. My family and I are convinced, but for those who may not yet be as certain, we offer this weight of evidence and encourage you to fearlessly obey even His slightest nudge.

CPSIA information can be obtained
at www.ICGtesting.com
Printed in the USA
LVHW102159110619
620927LV00009B/473/P